FIBIS Research Guides

C000181356

Researching Ancestors in the East India Company Armies

Peter A Bailey

With a Foreword by Ian Baxter

Families In British India Society   FIBIS Research Guide No.1

Cover illustration
Recruitment poster for the East India Company Armies

From the Collection at Blair Castle, Perthshire, reproduced by courtesy of the Trustees of the Blair Charitable Trust

The Families in British India Society (FIBIS)
Registered charity (No.1072403)
Established in 1998 to support persons seeking to study their ancestors' lives in India

FIBIS website: www.fibis.org

British Library Cataloguing in Publication Data
A catalogue record for this book is available from The British Library

ISBN 0-9547-116-1-0

Typeset and printed in Great Britain by Athenaeum Press, Gateshead

Contents

Contents

Contents

Foreword

Until quite recently the records of the East India Company's European armies in India (1748-1861) were less well served with respect to finding aids than the records of their counterparts in India, the British Army. Since then the balance has been redressed by the basic reference works of Farrington, Moir and Baxter (see page 2), and now Peter Bailey's present work takes the process several steps further. He has provided a thoroughgoing analysis of the relevant biographical sources together with an informed commentary and a series of useful tables and appendices. As might be expected his work relates mainly to the India Office Records (IOR) where the great bulk of the relevant material is to be found but he has not overlooked material elsewhere (see pages 66 and 83-86).

A valuable feature of his book is his provision of precise film references for the biographical material microfilmed at the India Office Records by the Church of Jesus Christ of Latter Day Saints (LDS). Those films, which cover most of the IOR biographical sources, are available for public consultation at LDS Family History Centres in the United Kingdom and elsewhere.

In his arrangement of the work the author has conveniently separated records relating to 'officers' from those relating to 'soldiers'. 'Officers' in this context means not only regular officers but surgeons and veterinary surgeons, 'soldiers' covers other ranks, NCOs, warrant officers and departmental officers. He has also included much useful material relating to pensions and wills. It should be noted that the Registers of the Military Family Pension Funds (see pages 60-62) are a very convenient source of information on officers' families and researchers should always consult them first before proceeding to more general sources such as Ecclesiastical Returns (IOR 'N' series) and Directories.

All in all, Peter Bailey's book should prove an essential reference tool for genealogical researchers, whether they are concerned merely to complete a family tree, or to go further and investigate their ancestors' lives in India in some depth.

Ian A Baxter

July 2006

Preface

This book is dedicated to the Officers and Soldiers of the former East India Company's Armies, i.e. pre-1861, and in particular to the Author's two ancestors who played a modest but necessary part in them.

It is greatly to be regretted that the proverbial 'mists of time' are causing the memories of these three armies rapidly to fade. Yet the bravery and exploits of the men who gave so much of their effort, and not infrequently their lives, in the creation and maintenance of the Empire's 'Jewel in the Crown' feature high in the annals of British soldiery. It is hoped that this work will assist those researching their ancestors who served in these armies and that this will aid their exploits to remain alive in the memory of the British people. Fortunately their legacies and traditions have been largely transferred today to the twenty-first century armies of Bangladesh, India and Pakistan. Long may these traditions continue into the future.

I offer three words of caution. Firstly, the India Office Records at the British Library, to which most of this work refers, are estimated to occupy 15 km. of shelf space! Despite the excellence of the cataloguing, particularly of the military records by Mr. Anthony Farrington, their former curator, there may just be some important records that I have overlooked.

Secondly, in selecting and recording both these records and the equivalent films made by the Genealogical Society of Utah (Church of Jesus Christ of Latter Day Saints), it is possible that some errors have crept in. As always in this type of work, all readers are advised to check the original references before engaging their time and costs.

Thirdly, as its title indicates, this book is about the East India Company's Armies. It does not deal with the regiments of the British Army which were always to be found serving alongside those of the Company.

Finally, I should like to express my gratitude to my colleagues in the Families in British India Society for assistance, advice and help with the checking of this book. In particular, I thank Ian Baxter and Richard Morgan. I would also like to thank Anthony Farrington for commenting on the text, and Alan Clibbery for his help with preparing the map. But my deepest gratitude goes to David Blake for his special contribution and forbearance during the final preparation of the book for publication and for making the arrangements for its publication, and to Lawrie Butler for undertaking so meticulously the burdensome task of proof reading the entire text.

It is also appropriate to thank both the India Office Records, custodian of essentially all the records cited, and the Latter Day Saints (LDS), for their support and encouragement in the course of my researches.

Peter Bailey

Chairman
Families in British India Society
July 2006

1. Introduction

This book is not an academic work on the history of India, nor even of the armies of the East India Company or of the Crown who served there. Its purpose is to assist the family historian with military ancestors who lived and served in the armies of the Honourable East India Company (HEIC) in India or its associated territories. It should enable a structured approach to research to be undertaken by those engaged in establishing their pedigree. For those interested in going further, it should point them towards obtaining some background to the social and domestic aspects of their ancestors' lives.

Thus, with the family historian in mind, the book's style is largely that of a list of useful records, plus included examples of what is to be found in the records themselves. It is believed that the mode of presentation of the records will enable a researcher to follow the logical sequence of events in the life of an ancestor who served in any one of the three EIC Armies.

It must immediately be acknowledged that by far the largest collection of resources available for research into the family history of both officers and men who served in the armies of the Honourable East India Company is lodged in the 'India Office Records' (IOR) in the Asian and African Studies Reading Room at the British Library at St. Pancras in London. All references given in this book are those of the IOR, unless alternatives are specifically recorded. The catalogue numbers quoted are generally fully comprehensive. Furthermore, many of these catalogues are becoming increasingly available on the 'Access to Archives' (A2A) web-site at www.a2a.org.uk. For anyone interested in using the India Office Records, a preliminary search in the A2A web-site is strongly recommended. It can save much valuable time once you have learned how to use it, particularly as in many cases searching the A2A is less laborious than searching the manual catalogues.

Most fortunately, the Families in British India Society (FIBIS) and others are transcribing many of the records themselves for publication either on the British Library web-site or on their own. Furthermore, the Church of Jesus Christ of Latter Day Saints (LDS) has microfilmed a large number of these records and is pleased to make them available to researchers at their Family History Centres at very modest cost. Reference is made to these microfilms wherever possible and appropriate throughout this guide.

Researchers wishing to understand and investigate the cataloguing of these records in greater depth are recommended to consult: *Guide to the Records of the India Office Military Department, IOR L/MIL and L/WS* by Anthony Farrington, British Library 1982. A more general guide to the records as a whole is given in *A General Guide to the India Office Records* by Martin Moir, British Library 1988. A less detailed but much more practical guide to most records with strong biographical content is *Baxter's Guide – Biographical Sources in the India Office Records* by Ian A. Baxter, 3rd Edition published by the 'Families in British India Society', 2004.

Please note that for simplicity throughout this document, and to distinguish them from officers, the term 'Soldier' is used to mean Non-Commissioned Officers and 'Other Ranks'. It is realized, of course, that officers strictly qualify for inclusion under the term 'Soldier'. The structure and presentation of the records in this guide are such as to progress logically through time. That is, a man's career passes from Recruitment to Training to Embarkation, to Appointment in India. It then moves to his Service in India, through Marriage, Baptism of any children to Discharge or Retirement and receipt of Pension to Death and to disposal of any Estate in India. The major records are split firstly into those pertaining to officers only and then those pertaining to soldiers. Further on, we consider those records which are common to both officers and soldiers.

Finally, virtually all these records must be viewed either at the IOR Section of the British Library or at an LDS Family History Centre and each is equipped with comprehensive catalogues. Much of the purpose of this book is, therefore, to familiarize the reader with the information that is available at these locations and to save precious time browsing for it.

2. India Office Records Catalogue Numbers and LDS Film Numbers

A major purpose of this work is the presentation both of the IOR Catalogue Numbers and the corresponding LDS Film Number of the particular record under discussion to enable researchers to identify the record for which they are looking as simply and rapidly as possible. The sequencing of IOR catalogue numbers is fully logical and retains priority both because of this logicality and because the IOR are guardians of the original records.

Originally, the records were the property of the East India Company and were retained in their archives at East India House in Leadenhall Street in London. When the Company's authority in India passed to the Crown in 1858, these records were transferred to the newly established India Office although, regrettably, many of them were deemed unworthy of retention and were destroyed. In 1947 they were passed to what eventually became the Foreign and Commonwealth Office. In 1982, they were placed in the custody of the British Library, India Office Records (IOR) where they now remain. Access to them is freely available subject only to the obtaining of a Reader's Ticket, which is generally provided upon presentation of proof of identity and of sufficient justification of interest, and signature.

The LDS, or more correctly the Genealogical Society of Utah (GSU), are well known and highly appreciated around the world for the enormous value of the filming work that they undertake and, in particular, for making their records available to the public at large. The vast volume of the information collected and the rate at which this is growing must militate somewhat against the clarity of its presentation. It is therefore no criticism of the value of their work, to remark that the numbering sequence of their films is frequently discontinuous. This means that it is often not possible to establish a one-to-one correspondence between a given IOR reference series and a particular continuous run of LDS Film Numbers. Furthermore, the film titles in the LDS catalogues are often rather different than the IOR titles used in this book. Do not therefore be surprised if an LDS number produces some strangely titled films! The contents should still be as described in this book.

The films are made available at very modest cost, at most of the LDS's Family History Centres around the world, generally within two weeks of their being ordered there. The helpful staff may advise over the telephone which films should be ordered but it is preferable that the numbers be checked in their catalogue available at their FHCs or on their web-site at: www.familysearch.org

In this work, we use the IOR record sequence as the standard and endeavour to indicate the equivalent LDS Film Number alongside. For those records indicated by experience to be the more important and valuable, we present the complete sequence of the references to both sources. For records judged to be less important, we present summaries of both types of reference. From this there may be a temptation to deduce the precise reference in both sources by interpolation. Whereas this is often possible – though by no means always – with the IOR series, it is very frequently not possible for the LDS Film numbers. So, great care is advised. This is the case, in particular, for the most frequently consulted records of all. These are the formidable lists of indexes and actual records of Baptisms, Marriages and Burials.

For the many records not listed in full in this book, an LDS Film Number is provided which is known to be included in the list of film numbers forming the range used by the LDS to cover the series in question. It is then recommended that the reader visit the LDS website catalogue and insert this film number into its search function. This will lead to the presentation of the whole range of film numbers covering the series to be consulted and the easier selection of the film to order.

I make no great apology for proposing such a procedure. It would be impossible to have included every record of every series in a brief guide such as this. The LDS Catalogue is available at their various Family History Centres around the world and on their web-site at: www.familysearch.org.

Given the very large number of references included in this Guide, the lack of one-to-one correspondence between references to the original and to the film, and despite several detailed checks, it is possible that several errors remain. Readers are therefore strongly advised to check for themselves either in the IOR catalogues or in the 'familysearch' catalogues the details of any piece or film before placing an order.

Sources

It may be helpful to note here the IOR catalogue series most relevant to research of Officer and Soldier ancestors and the background to their lives. The two main series are:

- **Military Records**, L/MIL/-
- **Accountant General's Records**, L/AG/-

Both are listed in some detail in the List of Principal Sources at the end of this Guide.

Other relevant series are:

B	Minutes of the Court of Directors.
D	Auditors' References
E	Despatches to India
F	Despatches from India
L/MAR/-	Ships' Journals (Logs)
N	Ecclesiastical Indexes
P	Proceedings

3. Historical Background

The East India Company always insisted that its presence in India and South Asia was for the purposes of trade. It was always reluctant to sanction territorial expansion, although did not disclaim the profits that territorial acquisition brought with it.

The Charter to represent the Crown's merchant interests and to establish trade east of the Cape of Good Hope was granted by England's Queen Elizabeth in 1600. Naturally, the company's ships and trading posts (factories) in the East would have had to defend themselves from pirates, marauders and hostile powers of Europe and the East. For this purpose a number of mercenaries, both European and native, were initially both formally and informally engaged and equipped with arms. European gentlemen were, of course, generally commissioned as officers and previous military experience was an advantage. However, it should be remembered that the concept of 'standing armies' was highly unpopular in England in the seventeenth century, and a formally trained officer class was not available. This had changed by the time of the Continental wars of the early 18th century. Indexed and unindexed references to EIC military officers in the 17th and early 18th centuries may generally only be found in the Minutes of the Court of Directors (IOR Series B).

The Company's 'enlisted men' were frequently drawn from the local Indian population or the mixed Portuguese-Indian community who, because of their colour, were referred to as 'Topaz'.

It was the onset of war with the French in Europe in the mid-18th century, and its extension into India, which provoked the Company to appreciate the need to establish a more formal and expanded military stance in the East. It therefore recruited both European officers and soldiers for service in India and the records of both, available to family historians, largely date from this period.

By the dates of these wars the Company had divided its possessions into the following four areas, or 'Presidencies', each centred on its major trading centres. These were:

a. **Bengal Presidency** (centred at Fort William, Calcutta) founded in 1690.
b. **Bombay Presidency** (Bombay) brought to King Charles II by his Portuguese wife, Catherine of Braganza, as part of her dowry and given to the Company in 1668.
c. **Madras Presidency** (Fort St. George), founded in 1640.
d. **Bencoolen** (Fort York, founded in 1685 and renamed Fort Marlborough in 1714, in Sumatra), was a presidency from 1759 to 1803.

In addition, the Company owned the Atlantic Island of St. Helena, which it required to garrison.

Each Presidency was equipped with its own army and, when Fort Marlborough was 'exchanged' for Malacca with the Dutch in March 1824, and implemented in April 1825, the remaining three presidencies retained their separate armies until 1861, following the Company's effective demise. Although there were a few instances in which individual soldiers transferred from one army to another, in general these armies were quite separate. Nevertheless, they respected the same regulations and disciplines, laid down by the English Parliament, which were identical to, or very similar to, those of the army of the Crown.

On many occasions the army of one presidency would fight in the territory of another, sometimes alone and sometimes alongside the army of that territory itself. In particular, it is helpful to remember that the native soldiers of the Bengal Army objected to voyage at sea and could not be persuaded to serve overseas. Thus, although Burma and the 'Straits Settlements' (i.e. Penang, also known as Prince of Wales Island, Malacca and Singapore) were politically part of the Bengal Presidency, troops from Madras generally garrisoned those areas and fought there when appropriate. Furthermore, Aden was part of the Bombay Presidency and, again, troops of the Madras Presidency helped to garrison Aden.

Table 1 gives a list of the dates of the passing of the major Indian territories into British (East India Company) hands until, following the 'Great Mutiny', the India Act of 1858 transferred them to the Crown.

Table 2 provides a list of the major wars, with their three more important battles, undertaken by the East India Company's Armies from 1741 to 1861.

The map on the back cover of this Guide shows the territory under British control by 1858. It will be seen that the expansion took place mainly from Bengal into the north west and that area together with Assam and Burma came under the Bengal Presidency for military and ecclesiastical purposes.

4. The Structure of the East India Company's Armies

Evidently, the size and shape of the company's armies varied over time as their activities became more sophisticated and their responsibilities more widespread. One may consider these armies to have had their origins at the time of Clive in the 1750s and, although regimental structure based on that used by the British Army was rapidly established, there was a degree of flexibility in their overall organization. Despite the obvious success of these armies in establishing and maintaining the British as the predominant European power in India, a formal review of structure was considered necessary in the late 18th century. This was largely due to the threats posed by the designs of the new French Directory and of Napoleon Bonaparte.

A landmark in the structure of the three Presidential Armies was established in 1795. In that year the Government's Board of Control for the Affairs of India, included Henry Dundas who, not necessarily co-incidentally, was also Britain's Minister for War. Times were turbulent and the Company sought the advice of Dundas in the reorganization of its armies in India. It was the organization resulting from this advice that set the pattern for the Company's armies and which aided them in their conquest of much of the sub-continent over the following sixty years.

Table 3 summarizes the structure and its development over this sixty-year period for the major corps of the regular Presidency armies. It may be known that India additionally spawned a number of 'Irregular' units, some of which gained celebrity, e.g. 'Skinner's Horse'. Some of them became absorbed into the formal structure of the Company's armies, particularly in Bengal. Others remained irregular but frequently assisted the Company in its military endeavours. Few formal records exist of the latter and they are not considered here.

Although the ranks, numbers and structures of the various units changed somewhat over time, the typical structure of each major unit is indicated in Table 4.

Throughout the Company era, all officers and non-commissioned officers of European regiments were European. The senior officers, plus a number of senior non-commissioned officers of both the Native Infantry and Native Cavalry regiments were European. A number of native officers and native non-commissioned officers also served with these units. The majority of European officers were attached to the large number of Native Infantry (N.I.) regiments. Others, often with special training in England before embarking for India, were assigned to the European Infantry, Artillery and Engineering corps. With the passage of time officers, and some N.C.O.s, were detached for duty in 'support' roles such as 'Department of Public Works', Gun Carriage Manufactories, Ordnance Supply, etc. and later to Telegraph and Railway supervisory works. A number were provided by the Company to train and retain links with the armies of several of the 'Princely States'.

A Note about the Bengal European Cavalry.

Prior to the Mutiny, the Bengal Army included eight regiments of Native Cavalry. These were among the first to mutiny and, of course, to be disbanded.

Because of the effectiveness of Cavalry in the pursuit and operations against the mutineers, the Government gave orders for the recruitment of four regiments of European Cavalrymen in England. This was relatively rapidly achieved and the first of them became operational towards the middle of 1858.

When the Company Army was transferred to that of the Crown, these regiments were consolidated into three and became Her Majesty's 19th, 20th and 21st Hussars

Those interested in further study of the development of the Company armies' regimental structures are recommended to read, for example, *The Indian Army* by Boris Mollo (Poole, Blandford, 1981) and *A Register of Titles of the Units of the EIC and Indian Armies, 1666-1947* by Chris Kempton (Bristol, British Empire & Commonwealth Museum, Research Paper No. 1, c1997).

A Note about St. Helena

The East India Company took over the mid-South Atlantic island of St. Helena in 1659 in order that it might use slave labour to work on plantations there for the provision of fresh food for its ships. Also it acted as a mustering location for ships returning from the East so that they could sail in convoy through the sometimes dangerous waters of the North Atlantic.

Following restitution after an attack by the Dutch in 1672, a significant military garrison was established there for the island's defence. Such a garrison was typically composed of three companies of Artillery, three companies of Infantry and one Invalid company. Annual Muster Lists are available in IOR series L/MIL/13/1-14 which cover the period 1789 to 1834, when ownership of the island passed to the Crown and the garrison transferred to detachments of the British Army. One final 'Muster List', L/MIL/13/15 gives details of Pensioners,

Invalids and soldiers opting to remain on the island rather than returning to England.

Although the majority of recruits were sent out directly from England, a significant minority came from various corps of the Company's armies in India and from a variety of irregular military bodies in South Africa.

A Note about Bencoolen

In 1684 the Company established a formal trading post in Bencoolen on the west coast of Sumatra, constructing a fortification there, Fort York, with a military garrison for its protection. The site chosen proved unsatisfactory and, in 1714, a new one was established a few miles away and named Fort Marlborough. Apart from the years 1719-1723, the Company continued in occupation until 1825 when, in effect, the colony was exchanged with the Dutch for Malacca.

Records of the soldiers who garrisoned Forts York and Marlborough are rather sparse in the formal military section of the IOR. Embarkation Lists for officers and recruits can be found in the L/MIL/9/85-99 records in the same way as for the three main presidencies as described in Section 10.3 below. However, as far as has been found, the only service records available are nominal rolls for the years 1708, 1716 and 1731 among the Bombay Presidency records in L/MIL/12/117-118.

Beyond these, references to officers and soldiers are listed by Alan Harfield in his excellent book *Bencoolen – A History of the Honourable East India Company's Garrison on the West Coast of Sumatra, 1685-1825* (A & J Partnership, 1995). He has evidently assembled these lists after painstakingly trawling through IOR series E, G, H, I and L/P&S. The book is on the open shelves of the Asia, Pacific and African Reading Room at the British Library, under reference OIR 354.598.

5. The Demise of the East India Company's Armies

During the Mutiny in 1857-9, the British Parliament passed the 'Government of India Act' of 1858. This removed the charter from the Company and gave the administration of British possessions in India and South Asia to the Crown. This responsibility was exercised through a new 'Secretary of State for India' who replaced both the Company itself and the Board of Control as the home authority supervising the Government of India. The latter was left largely untouched, although the Governor-General added the more ornamental title of Viceroy to his existing designation. The Company's European regiments transferred to the Crown to become part of the British Army.

Officers of the East India Company Armies held their commissions from the Crown. They could, in effect, resign at any time. At the time of the winding up of the Company's armies a few did resign. Those in Field or Staff positions tended to continue for some years in much the same capacity as before but after some years the system was deemed to have become 'top heavy' and many were urged to resign. Officers commanding European regiments generally remained with them and so transferred to the British Army.

It was largely the regiments of the Bengal Native Infantry and Native Cavalry that mutinied in 1857 and thought was given to the avoidance of similar problems in the future. The ratio of Indian to British soldiers in India at the time of the Mutiny, had been as much as five or six to one. Henceforward it was to be a maximum of only two to one in Bengal and three to one in Madras and Bombay, with allowance for the presence of several British Army regiments. Also, the Company's system of permanent allocation of each of its Native Infantry officers to a particular regiment was discontinued: officers were 'pooled' into a 'Staff Corps' and allocated to native regiments of the newly established 'Indian Army' in each presidency. However, fewer regiments meant the need for fewer officers and many were seconded to other duties in the Indian Police, the Political Service or general administration.

In preparation for the re-organization, each soldier was given the choice of transfer to the British Army, or discharge without pension, but with a bounty. The exercise took some two years to complete and very roughly half of the soldiers selected each option. Thus, although each regiment or battalion transferred, it was much depleted in numbers. Table 5 details the relations between the old Company and the new British Army nomenclature.

A number of men were given the option to transfer to the new 'Indian Army'. This generally applied to some officers and soldiers of more senior rank. They were to provide the officer class of the Cavalry and Infantry units of the Indian Army. Others, generally N.C.O.s, were selected to transfer to the 'Unattached List' (UL), which mirrored the former 'Town Major's List'. In the UL, they mainly worked in the Commissariat Department, which was responsible in general for transport, supplies and support both to the British and Indian armies, the Department of Public Works (DPW) or the Ordnance Department. A few transferred to diverse posts such as Viceroy's bandsmen, drill instructors, laboratory serjeants, etc. Although outside the scope of this guide, it may be mentioned that the Government of India generally continued the system of Muster Lists for these soldiers, which had been established by the Company.

6. Officers' Career Patterns

In late Georgian and Victorian England it was usual for the eldest son of a gentleman to follow in his father's footsteps and to take over his father's estate. Younger sons would join the army or the Church. With the expansion of Empire, and given the opportunities to gain a reputation and honour for the family, a young man was frequently urged by his father to join the army. In many cases, the family was unable to support the necessary cost of purchasing a commission in the British Army for a second son but might manage to set him up as a cadet in the armies of the East India Company. This would commonly be the case amongst the comparatively poor Scottish and Anglo-Irish gentry, and even persons of Huguenot ancestry, who were a hard-working and ambitious group rising in society, but still self-consciously separate, in the eighteenth century. This accounts for the relatively large numbers of these people amongst the Company's Officer class. Entry was initially at a minimum age of 15, later raised to 16 years, when idealism is usually high.

Officer Cadets were generally recruited by recommendation and sponsorship by a member of the Company's Court of Directors or a Member of the Board of Control. In the early years of the Company armies they were sent directly to India to receive training there. However, from the late 18th century the Company paid for 'specialist' training in the British Army facilities in England alongside the future British Army officers. This applied to officers destined for service in the Artillery (Woolwich) or in Engineering (Chatham). Such an arrangement eventually proved too expensive and, from 1809 onwards, they were sent for this specialist education at the Company's own newly established Military Seminary at Addiscombe, in Surrey. From 1816 onwards, most other cadets could opt to be sent to Addiscombe. Others choosing to be sent directly to India, were styled 'Direct Cadets'. Interestingly, towards the end of the 18th century, some Directors were found to be 'selling' recommendations. Cornwallis put a stop to this!

It is not always obvious how a particular cadet was allocated to a particular presidency. Preferences were taken into account, particularly if the cadet already had some family connection with one of the presidencies. Many cadets specified, with their application, to which presidency they wished to be sent. Otherwise, one supposes that they were allocated on the basis of need. Upon 'passing out' they embarked for India where, upon arrival, they were appointed to their future regiment and were accorded the rank of 'Ensign' ('Cornet' for Cavalry). It was usual for a man to remain with this same regiment throughout his career or until he may have risen to Staff Rank, although a small number were appointed to 'extra-regimental' positions when they demonstrated a particular ability – or had the right connections! At some time in his career an officer might have been selected to undertake special activities for the Government. In this latter capacity, he would temporarily be 'detached' from his regiment whilst engaged on such activity.

It must again be emphasized that promotion through the ranks for an officer was strictly by seniority. When several Cadets passed out at the same time, the higher the marks gained by an individual in the exam, the higher was his seniority.

It was sometimes the practice to establish seniority of such cadets by considering their dates of appointment to be on successive days. Although there was no official 'purchase of commissions', such as was practised in the British Army, a senior officer in a Company regiment expected to be 'paid' to resign when his time to do so was approaching. This procedure was sometimes sufficient to encourage an officer to resign early, thereby accelerating the occurrence of the vacancy and making way for the officer next in seniority to replace him. Then, of course, all the remaining officers could move up a 'step'. In order to facilitate this 'step' process, as it was known, all of the junior officers contributed to the necessary fund to hasten the resignation. This practice, although never officially approved by the authorities, was tacitly condoned as a way of speeding up the promotion process.

It may be remarked that many officers were appointed to 'Brevet' rank. In many instances there were insufficient vacancies in a particular corps for an officer to be promoted to the next higher rank after serving a considerable time at the lower rank. In such cases this might be recognized by his receiving from the presidency military command a letter or 'brevet' (French word for letter) recognizing him as promoted to the higher rank in the army whereas he had to remain at his current rank in the regiment until an appropriate vacancy had arisen. In other words, the officer concerned held a higher 'Army Rank' than his 'Regimental Rank'. Notwithstanding this, he was permitted to wear the uniform of the brevet rank and to retain it if and when he retired.

Officers were granted furlough from time to time and were permitted to return to England with pay for three years after service in India of ten years. Prior to 1795, they had to obtain special permission from the Company to rejoin the service in India. After 1795, they could be granted furlough with the right to return. After 1818 and for urgent reasons, an officer with less than ten years service could be granted furlough to Europe for one year, but without pay. By their late twenties, they had been promoted to a rank and a salary which enabled them to support a wife. Much of their furlough in England, Australia or elsewhere would, therefore, be spent in finding a young lady who would be willing to suffer the rigours of life with him in India. It is worth mention that, if an officer took his furlough before rounding the Cape, he remained on full pay, whereas if he travelled on to England, he went on to half-pay. The Cape, with its temperate climate and abundance of hospitable people with marriageable daughters, became a favourite place for furlough and many officers married South African ladies. Anyone who cannot find an officer's marriage in Britain or India is advised to consider looking in South Africa.

Following an Act of Parliament in 1813 restricting the powers of the Company, young ladies, suitably chaperoned by a female relative or friend, would join the 'fishing fleet' and travel to India in search of a husband from among the officer class. If an officer became ill, or was lightly wounded, he would be permitted local leave, at a more comfortable resort by the sea or at a cooler 'hill station' until pronounced fit to resume duty. A senior Medical Officer could recommend sick leave to Europe at any time.

The subject of 'Batta' is worth mentioning here. Batta was an allowance made to Officers and Soldiers for special service such as when in the field, on the march or whilst undertaking duties far from their usual station. Originally granted only on occasions, awards of batta became more and more an expectation, particularly by officers, who were in a better position to insist upon its payment than soldiers. Thus batta became a source of friction between officers and their superiors who were endeavouring to adopt measures of economy from time to time. Formal awards of batta for war service are listed on page 68.

An officer was permitted to resign for a large number of reasons. These included coming into a significant inheritance, illness or serious wounding or, occasionally, as a device to avoid the potential disgrace of a court martial. However, life as an officer became progressively better as he climbed through the ranks and so early resignation was not frequently pursued. The dangers presented by the climate, disease and battle were ever present but not generally officially cited as reasons for resignation. Nevertheless, they may well sometimes have been the case, possibly under pressure from the officers' wives. Thus, although a limited number of officers were cashiered for 'conduct unbecoming an officer and a gentleman', or even for a more serious crime, officers would pursue their careers until they could find a reason to return home to live out the rest of their years on a comfortable pension.

7. Officers' Entry into Service

In the Crown's Army commissions could be purchased and, for example, a combination of wealth and patronage caused the future Duke of Wellington to have been a Regimental Colonel at the age of 27. In the Company's Armies, officers were promoted by seniority only. However, in order to have been accepted into the Army as a Cadet in the first place, an applicant required recommendation by a person of good situation, local to his place of birth or long-term residence, and to have been sponsored by a Member of the Company's Court of Directors or of the Board of Control. This is reflected in the 'Cadet Papers' described below.

7.1. Records Prior to 1775

Appointments as officers or cadets in the Company's armies were the prerogative of the Court of Directors. Thus, prior to the establishment of separate and specific records, details of such appointments are to be found in the Minutes of the Court of Directors, series B in the India Office Records. Entries are generally reported to the authorities in India via the *Despatches to India*, IOR series E/4. The LDS has not filmed these records.

The gap between 1775 and 1789, may be covered by the 'Cadet Registers' (Section 7.4.)

7.2. Applications for Entry - Cadet Papers 1789-1860

These 'Cadet Papers' cover the years 1789 to 1860. They include, importantly, justification of the applicant's age in the form of a certified extract from the baptismal register or affidavit of some local dignitary to whom he is known. Information useful to the genealogist, included in these documents, are dates and places of birth plus names of parents. Additionally, there may be reference to his schooling and letters of recommendation, crucially by one of the Company Directors. These are the earliest separate records of the recruitment of officers and are to be found in IOR 'Cadet Papers', references L/MIL/9/107 to 253. Although these are particularly important records, it is not feasible to include all 146 in this document. Readers are advised to follow the procedures below during a visit to the IOR, or a local LDS Family History Centre.
A nominal index to these documents is available in the IOR Reading Room, with reference Z/L/MIL/9/1, and in LDS Film No. 1886143 (Item 1) or Film No. 1912072 (Item 1). The index provides the Cadets' names listed alphabetically, followed by the volume and folio numbers containing his actual papers. The information in the index from an example taken at random, is in the form:

De La Motte, Charles Digby   178/27 - 33

This means that this cadet should be sought in L/MIL/9/178, folios 27 to 33. Researchers using the LDS films are advised to insert either of the above film numbers into the LDS catalogue which will bring up the whole range of films covering the Cadet papers. The LDS catalogue lists the contents of each film in the form:

1831-1832, 178   1832-1833, 179   1833-1834, 180/1-357   FHL BRITISH Film 1951923

which means that L/MIL/9/178 covering the season 1831-1832 is on film 1951923.

An alternative means of discovering that L/MIL/9/178 is the volume containing De La Motte's cadet papers, is to use the A2A website: enter De La Motte in the keyword box, and select British Library, Asia, Pacific and Africa Collections in the Location Box.

The information provided for De la Motte in the Cadet Papers themselves is:

Example of an Application for Selection as an Officer Cadet

Addiscombe – Season 1831

The humble petition of *Charles Digby de la Motte* sheweth that your petitioner is desirous of entering the Military Service of the Company as a Cadet for the Military Seminary, to which he has been nominated by *John G. Ravenshaw*, Esq. at the recommendation of *Peter de la Motte*, Esq. and should he be so fortunate as to appear to your Honours eligible for that station promises to conduct himself with fidelity and honour.

Director's Nomination

I, *John Goldsborough Ravenshaw*, Esq., being one of the Directors of the East India Company beg leave to present the Petitioner *Charles Digby de la Motte* as Cadet for the Military Seminary as one of my nominations for the season *1831* provided he shall appear to you eligible for that station; and I do declare that from the character given of him by his father *Colonel de la Motte* who certifies that he is well acquainted with his family, character and connexions, he is in my opinion a fit person to petition the East India Company for the appointment he now solicits.

Rec'd to me by	Examined and passed the	Signed *John G. Ravenshaw*
His father	*25th January 1832* by me:	East India House *25th Jany 1832*

(As part of the necessary justification of age and baptism, there are then included:)

These are to certify to all whom it doth or may concern that the Court of Directors of the United Company of Merchants trading to the East Indies have received from their Government at Bombay a paper entitled "Registers of Baptism on Bombay & at Subordinates Commencing from 1st January and ending to Ultimo November 1816" signed N. Wade, Senior Chaplain and in which paper I find the following entry:

1816, May 20th Charles Digby, son of Peter de la Motte, Captain in the H.C. Military Service by Sophia his wife Rev N. Wade.

Where & When born: Bombay, 7th Jan 1816.

In witness whereof I hereunto set my hand at the East India House in London this (blank) day of January in the year of our Lord 1832.

Signed: William Carter.

Applications for Officer Cadets (Continued)

The Answers to the following questions must be written by the Cadet himself, in the presence of one of the Clerks of the Cadet Office:

1. What is your Name?
    Charles Digby de la Motte

2. At what school have you been educated?
    Mr. Wade's, Slough, near Windsor

3. Of what nature has your education been?
    Classical & Mathematical

4. What is the professional, situation & residence of your parents or next of kin?
    My father, Col. In the Bombay Army, resides at Exmouth, Devonshire.

5. Who recommended you to Mr. Ravenshaw?
    Colonel De La Motte – My Father.

6. Do you believe that any person has received or is to receive any pecuniary benefit on account of your nomination?
    I do not believe any person has received any pecuniary consideration.

7. Are you aware that if it should be hereafter discovered that your appointment has been obtained by improper means that you will be dismissed and rendered ineligible to hold any situation in the Company's Service again?
    I am.

8. Are you likewise aware that if you omit to insure the amount of your passage and outfit at some one of the Public Offices, the Court, in the event of loss and damage by shipwreck, or other contingency will not attend to any application for indemnification?
    I am.

Signature of Cadet, his father and J.G. Ravenshaw

In case of sudden removal from the Seminary from sickness or other cause, the cadet is to be received by:

Mr. Hyndman, 22, Fludyer St. Westminster – or in his absence by:
Mr. Henry Cotes, 67, Sloane St.

(Also included are:)
Part 1 Formal Application to be signed by Cadet – not completed (Replaced by above)
Part 2 Formal Nomination by Director – not completed (Replaced by above)
Part 3 Extract from Parish Register of St. Thomas, Bombay
Part 4 Medical Certificate and affidavit of vaccination – signed by G. Hobson, Surgeon.
Included also are three letters indicating that the cadet has some academic inadequacy.

7.3 Training - Addiscombe Military Seminary

In the early days of the Company Armies, cadets were sent 'direct' to India to train either with the regiments to which they were appointed, or for a limited period (1802 – 1816), in special colleges established in India. Then the Company came to recognize that specialist training was needed for cadets destined for its technical branches. From 1798 it paid for its Artillery and Engineering Cadets to be trained with those of the King's Army at the Royal Military Academies at Woolwich and Chatham. This later proved to be very expensive and in 1809 the Court of Directors sanctioned the establishment of a special 'Seminary Committee' and opened its own seminary at Addiscombe in Surrey for the purpose of providing such specialist training for its own cadets. Later still, other cadets were trained at Addiscombe before being sent to India, if it was judged that they required it.

Records of cadets at Addiscombe fall into two broad classes. Firstly, there are the Cadet Registers classified by season of joining, viz:

Season Range	IOR Reference	LDS Film No.
1809 – 1818	L/MIL/9/333	1867022
1819 – 1836	L/MIL/9/334	1867022
1836 – 1852	L/MIL/9/335	1867022
1852 – 1861	L/MIL/9/336	1867093

Secondly, there are series of Monthly Reports on progress in Mathematics and Classics of cadets, not only at Addiscombe, but also those sent for additional specialist training at the Crown's Engineering Establishment at Chatham. These may be considered of less immediate genealogical importance but are to be found in L/MIL/9/339 to 355. The Catalogue in the IOR Reading Room will provide details of the years and content of each file.

The equivalent LDS Film Numbers are 1867093, 1885477 & 1885504. By typing one of these numbers into the LDS Catalogue 'Film/Fiche' Search procedure, the reader may find details of the years and contents of these three films.

7.4 Registers of Cadets and Assistant Surgeons

In addition to the foregoing, brief details of Cadets and Assistant Surgeons may be found in L/MIL/9/255 to 269 or LDS Films Nos. 1835744 to 1835746 and 1701739. It should be stated that the Company recognized the need for adequate medical support for its operations in India at least as early as 1764 and organized a formal Medical Service in 1788. From 1773, as for officer cadets, candidates for this service were nominated by Company Directors and had to provide certificates of age and testimonials as well as evidence of their medical qualifications. Once appointed, they were granted a commission as an Assistant Surgeon and could then progress in their career to the ranks of Surgeon, Surgeon Major and to Surgeon General.

A nominal index to the 'Assistant Surgeons Papers' is to be found on the IOR Reading Room open shelves in Z/L/MIL/9/5 and LDS Film No. 1886143 (or 1912072). These lead to the records themselves, which are:

1804 – 1805	L/MIL/9/358 sequentially through to:
1854	L/MIL/9/396

But, unfortunately, these records themselves were not filmed by the LDS.

Lists of Cadets and Assistant Surgeons appointed to each Presidency were also compiled annually. They are in alphabetical order and may be found in the records L/MIL/9/270 to 281 or LDS Films Nos. 1701739 and 1866880-81 These records are sequential but the dates are discontinuous and so they are detailed as follows:

Registers of Cadets and Assistant Surgeons

Presidency	Dates	IOR Reference	LDS Film No.
Bengal	1794 to 1814	L/MIL/9/270	1701739-40
	1808, 1811 & 1815-28	L/MIL/9/271	1701740
	1829 to 1854	L/MIL/9/272	1701740
	1854 to 1862	L/MIL/9/273	1701740
Madras	1794 to 1814	L/MIL/9/274	1701740
	1804-5, 1811, 1814-28	L/MIL/9/275	1701740
	1829 to 1854	L/MIL/9/276	1866880
	1854 to 1862	L/MIL/9/277	1866880
Bombay	1796 to 1814	L/MIL/9/278	1866880
	1811 & 1815-1828	L/MIL/9/279	1866880
	1829 to 1854	L/MIL/9/280	1866880
	1854 to 1862	L/MIL/9/281	1866881

In addition, useful material concerning the appointment of cadets, their ranking, ship of embarkation to India etc. may be found in 'Cadet Miscellaneous Papers' L/MIL/9/282 to 291 and LDS Film Nos. 1866881 and 1866882.

Similar material for Assistant Surgeons is to be found in L/MIL/9/397 to 408 but, again, no equivalent LDS Film is available.

7.5 Veterinary Surgeons

Evidently, the Company required Veterinary Surgeons for the care of the large numbers of horses used by its officers, its cavalry and its Horse Artillery. No doubt they saw service with the necessary elephants, bullocks and, occasionally, the camels in the Company's service also.

Application for service in India was made in the same way as by Cadets and Assistant Surgeons. In other words, they required to give proof of age and qualifications and had to be sponsored by a member of the Court of Directors. Papers, including the petitions, testimonials, proof of age etc. are to be found from 1826 to 1859 in IOR ref: L/MIL/9/433 and supplementary lists and data feature in L/MIL/9/434. It is not thought that these records have been filmed by the LDS.

8. Officers' Services

8. 1 'Official'* Full Records of Officers' Services

Each cadet was appointed to the service of one of the three Presidencies, Bengal, Madras or Bombay. With few exceptions, mainly in the earlier years of the Company, he would remain in the army of his appointed Presidency throughout his career and would be eligible for promotion strictly in order of seniority. Ability was not a factor!

The major and most rapidly available records providing a summary of each particular officer's service are to be found in the Presidency Service Army Lists. Alphabetical Indexes to these records may be found on the open shelves in the IOR Reading Room at the British Library or in the LDS microfilms as follows:

Bengal	Z/L/MIL/10/1	LDS Film No.: 1886143 Item 7
Madras	Z/L/MIL/11/1	LDS Film No.: 1886143 Item 11
Bombay	Z/L/MIL/12/1	LDS Film No.: 1886143 Item 14

Reference to these indexes is essential. Entries in the earlier grouping of these records follow no alphabetical or chronological order. From 1844 (Bengal) 1847 (Madras) and 1853 (Bombay) until they cease in 1859, the style changes and records for each officer are updated annually.

In the Index, each officer was initially given a series of three numbers to assist his location. The first is the Number of the Volume of his main, or initial, entry. The second is the folio number of his entry in that volume. The third number is effectively an 'Identification Number', which remains valid for all years of his subsequent service. He will then be found under this number in the relevant volumes covering this 'Identification Number' for subsequent years until his career is ended. Later, officers entering the service after the change to annual updating, will have only the single 'identification

Fortunately, these indexes are now available on the A2A web-site (www.a2a.org.uk) and it is strongly advised to commence the search for your man there. This search will bypass the complexities of the process described above and bring up all the relevant references.

The example of an 'Officer's Service' given on page 23 shows how valuable they are. However, it is important to note that, apart from a few elderly retired General Officers, who never technically retired, they do not include career details of officers who died or retired before 1830. For such officers you may occasionally find career details in 'Auditors' References, 1799-1835 (IOR Ref. D/153-252)

In view of the importance of these records to researchers, a detailed breakdown of them, together with an example of the information typically found, is given on pages 20-23.

---

* 'Official' records are those originally entered by the Company's Clerks as distinct from those appearing later in printed publications.

Records of Officers' Services Part A

	Bengal (1770-1843)		Madras (1762-1846)		Bombay (1770-1852)	
Index	Z/L/MIL/10/1	1886143 Item 7	Z/L/MIL/11/1	1886143 Item 11	Z/L/MIL/12/1	1886143 Item 14
Volume	IOR Reference	LDS Film No	IOR Reference	LDS Film No	IOR Reference	LDS Film No
1	L/MIL/10/20	1867211 Item 5	L/MIL/11/38	1885571	L/MIL/12/67	1966147
2	L/MIL/10/21	1867255	L/MIL/11/39	1885572	L/MIL/12/68	1966147
3	L/MIL/10/22	1885472 Item 3	L/MIL/11/40	1885572	L/MIL/12/69	1966147
4	L/MIL/10/23	1867255	L/MIL/11/41	1885572	L/MIL/12/70	1966147/8
5	L/MIL/10/24	1867255	L/MIL/11/42	1885573	L/MIL/12/71	1966148
6	L/MIL/10/25	1867256	L/MIL/11/43	1885573	L/MIL/12/72	1966148
7	L/MIL/10/26	1867256	L/MIL/11/44	1885573	L/MIL/12/73	1966148
8	L/MIL/10/27	1867256	L/MIL/11/45	1885574	L/MIL/12/74	1966148
9	L/MIL/10/28	1867257	L/MIL/11/46	1885574	L/MIL/12/75	1966148
10	L/MIL/10/29	1867257	L/MIL/11/47	1885574		
11	L/MIL/10/30	1867257	L/MIL/11/48	1885574		
12	L/MIL/10/31	1867257	L/MIL/11/49	1885574		
13	L/MIL/10/32	1867258				
14	L/MIL/10/33	1867258				
15	L/MIL/10/34	1867258				
16	L/MIL/10/35	1867258				

Records of Officers' Services

Part B: 1844 to 1858 (Bengal)

Presidency	Year	IOR Reference	Folio Number	LDS Film No.
Bengal	1844	L/MIL/10/36	1 – 328	1867258 Item 5
	1844	L/MIL/10/37	329-500	1867529 Item 1-2
	1845	L/MIL/10/38	1-328	1867529 Item 1-2
	1845	L/MIL/10/39	329-527	1885473 Item 1
	1846	L/MIL/10/40	1-328	1867259 Item 3
	1846	L/MIL/10/41	329-543	1867260
	1847	L/MIL/10/42	1-328	1867260
	1847	L/MIL/10/43	329-523	1867260
	1847	L/MIL/10/43	523-555	1867261
	1848	L/MIL/10/44	1-344	1867261
	1848	L/MIL/10/45	345-566	1867261
	1849	L/MIL/10/46	1-193	1867262
	1849	L/MIL/10/47	193-424	1867262
	1849	L/MIL/10/48	425-577	1867262
	1850	L/MIL/10/49	1-283	1867262
	1850	L/MIL/10/49	283-400	1867263
	1850	L/MIL/10/50	401-593	1867263
	1851	L/MIL/10/51	1-367	1867263*
	1851	L/MIL/10/51	367-424	1867264
	1851	L/MIL/10/52	425-606	1867264
	1852	L/MIL/10/53	1-433	1867264
	1852	L/MIL/10/54	434-621	1867287
	1853	L/MIL/10/55	1-412	1867287
	1853	L/MIL/10/55	412-435	1867288
	1853	L/MIL/10/56	436-633	1867288
	1854	L/MIL/10/57	1-240	1867288
	1854	L/MIL/10/58	241-450	1867288*
	1854	L/MIL/10/58	450-509	1867289
	1854	L/MIL/10/59	510-651	1867289
	1855	L/MIL/10/60	1-447	1867289*
	1855	L/MIL/10/61	447-665	1867290
	1856	L/MIL/10/62	1-473	1867290*
	1856	L/MIL/10/63	473-681	1867291
	1857	L/MIL/10/64	1-447	1867291
	1857	L/MIL/10/65	448-712	1867292
	1858	L/MIL/10/66	1-456	1867292
	1858	L/MIL/10/67	457-729	1867293

Reminder: Use the index of the relevant presidency to determine the IOR Reference Number and Folio Number of the first entry in which to find the officer's Record of Service, plus his 'Identification Number' for subsequent years of service. Better still, it is now possible to locate the references by using the A2A web-site and researchers are advised to consult this.

Records of Officers' Services

Part B: 1847 to 1859 (Madras) and 1853 to 1859 (Bombay)

Presidency	Year	IOR Reference	Folio Number	LDS Film No.
Madras	1847	L/MIL/11/50	1-387	1885575
	1848	L/MIL/11/51	1-279	1885575
	1848	L/MIL/11/52	280-389	1885575
	1849	L/MIL/11/53	1-375	1885575*
	1849	L/MIL/11/53	375-408	1885598
	1850	L/MIL/11/54	1-417	1885598
	1851	L/MIL/11/55	1-165	1885598*
	1851	L/MIL/11/55	165-321	1885599
	1851	L/MIL/11/56	321-425	1885599
	1852	L/MIL/11/57	1-430	1885599
	1853	L/MIL/11/58	1-438	1885600
	1854	L/MIL/11/59	1-390 (sic)	1885600
	1854	L/MIL/11/59	386-455	1885601
	1855	L/MIL/11/60	1-543	1885601
	1856	L/MIL/11/61	1-360	1885601*
	1856	L/MIL/11/61	360-475	1885602
	1857	L/MIL/11/62	1-320	1885602
	1857	L/MIL/11/63	321-491	1885602
	1858	L/MIL/11/64	1-380	1885603
	1858	L/MIL/11/65	381-506	1885603
	1859	L/MIL/11/66	432-519	1885603
Bombay	1853	L/MIL/12/76	1-257	1966149
	1854	L/MIL/12/77	1-266	1966149
	1855	L/MIL/12/78	1-196	1966149*
	1855	L/MIL/12/78	196-274	1966250
	1856	L/MIL/12/79	1-280	1966250
	1857	L/MIL/12/80	1-221	1966250*
	1857	L/MIL/12/80	221-294	1966251
	1858	L/MIL/12/81	1-299	1966251
	1859	L/MIL/12/82	1-238	1966251*
	1859	L/MIL/12/82	238-309	1966252 - Item 1

*Beware: Each folio is presented in two halves, with two officers on each half. In these instances, the LDS film gives half of the numbered folio at the end of one film and the second half at the beginning of the next. Accordingly, researchers seeking the folio numbers in which these splits occur are advised to order both films to ensure obtaining the correct entry.

Records of Officers' Services – Part C

Example of Details to be found in Officers' Services

Indexed in Z/L/MIL/10/2 in IOR Reading Room or LDS Film No. 1886143

ABBOTT, George, 15th Bengal N. I. from L/MIL/10/26 folio 3 (LDS Film No. 1867256)

Dates of Commissions as:
Ensign: 16 Jan 1824, 15th NI
Lieutenant: 13 May 1825,15th NI
Captain: 10 Jany. 1838 G.O. 15 Jan. 1838
Major:
Lt. Col.:
Colonel:

George Abbott – Nominated by R.C. Plowden Esq., at the recommendation of Cadet's mother, widow of G. E. Abbott, Esq. Born in India 26th Nov. 1803. Produced a warrant from the Duke of Wellington as a Cadet in the Royal Artillery. Arrived 19th May 1824. G.O. 22d do. – Shared Bhurtpore Prize Money as Lieut: (Prize Rolls). Leave for 4 months to Dinapore on UPA. G.O. 22d March 1827. Appointed to the Pioneers. G.O. 20th Aug 1828. Leave for 6 months to the Presidency on P.A. G.O. 6th Oct 1829. Leave for 3 months to remain at the Presidency and to join. G.O. 24th March 1830. To do duty with European Recruits in Fort William, G.O. 18th May 1830. Leave to enable him to rejoin his Corps from 1st Nov: at 20th Dec: G.O. 29th Nov. 1830. Requests that the Certificate of his having passed his public examinations at Woolwich may be returned to him if in the office of the Mily. Secretary to Govt., and is informed in reply that it has never been received. Cons: 21 June 1833. No.151. Has leave to Meerut on UPA from 25th Decr. 1833 till 25th March 1834, G.O. 7th Decr. 1833. Above leave cancelled by leave from 1st Feby. Till 31st Mar. 1834. The Regtl. Order of the 16th Ulto. Appointing him to act as Adjt. To his Corps confirmed – G.O. 17 April '37. Placed at the disposal of the President in Council, for the purpose of surveying the Post Road from Midnapore to Nagpore as far as Ryepore – G.O. 27 Nov '37 till: Cons. 29 Jan No. 73 & G.O. 21st Feby. '38. To receive during his employment on this Survey, in addition to his Mily. pay & allowances, the allowance of an Asst. Revenue Surveyor, Rs. 618 per mo., which aggregate sum was to include all charges of establishment.

Govt. Report that Lieut. Abbott shortly after taking charge fell a victim on 1st April '38 to the undertaking in consequence of the insalubrity of the locality in which he was compelled to proceed with the survey – India Pub. Cons. Sept. to Decr. '37 and Mil. Cons. 7 May '38, No. 209, and Pub. Letter from India 27 June '38, No. 20 (71). Proceedings relative to the Estate recorded on Mily. Cons. 30 April & 23 July '38, Nos. 154 & 198

[For abbreviations see p105]

8.2 'Official'* Summary Records of Officers' Services

Summaries of Officers' Services were compiled in 1834 and an alphabetical list of all officers serving from 1759 to 1834 (a) and of those still serving in 1843 (b) may be found as given below. Services for Medical Officers, compiled later, cover the whole of the periods as indicated.

For the period 1799-1835 a summary of service, compiled by the officer himself, may sometimes be found in the relevant pension records.

	IOR Reference	LDS Film Nos.
Bengal		
Army Officers	L/MIL/10/68(a) and 69(b)	1867293(a) and 1867294(b)
Medical Officers	L/MIL/10/70-74 (1765-1858)	1867294 (Dead/Retired)
		1867295 (Serving to 1858)
Madras		
Army Officers	L/MIL/11/67-68(a) and 69(b)	1885604 (a and b)
Medical Officers	L/MIL/11/70-72 (1760-1858)	1885605 (A-I) and 606 (I-Z)
Bombay		
Army Officers	L/MIL/12/83(a) and 84(b)	1966252 (a and b)
Medical Officers	L/MIL/12/85-86 (1788-1858)	1966252 (A-P) and 309 (R-Z)

Whereas the pre-1860 records of service usually provide a relatively detailed picture of an officer's career, there are additional, but less detailed, records established after 1860 when an officer was granted furlough to Europe. Strictly, these records apply to the Indian Army. However, as has been explained in Section 5, many officers transferred from the Company's Armies to the Indian Army and so the records will be relevant to your research, particularly in the earlier years.

Fortunately, these latter records also include details of the service of Surgeons and Assistant Surgeons and of Departmental and Warrant Officers, plus a number of senior NCOs. References are provided on the next page.

* 'Official' records are those originally entered by the Company's Clerks as distinct from those appearing later in printed publications.

Officers' Summary Service Lists (Established when the Officer was granted furlough in Europe)

		Bengal			Madras			Bombay	
Vo Index	Years	IOR Ref. Z/L/MIL/10/2	LDS Film 1886143	Years	IOR Ref. Z/L/MIL/11/2	LDS Film 1866143	Years	IOR Ref. Z/L/MIL/12/2	LDS Film 1886143
1	1860-62	L/MIL/10/75	1867336	1860-62	L/MIL/11/73	1885739	1860-62	L/MIL/12/88	1966309-10
2	1862-63	L/MIL/10/76	1867336	1862-67	L/MIL/11/74	1885739	1863-64	L/MIL/12/89	1966310
3	1863-65	L/MIL/10/77	1867337	1863	L/MIL/11/75	1885739-40	1864-66	L/MIL/12/90	1966310
4	1865-66	L/MIL/10/78	1867337	1863-64	L/MIL/11/76	1885740	1866-68	L/MIL/12/91	1966311
5	1866-68	L/MIL/10/79	1867337	1864-66	L/MIL/11/77	1885740	1868-70	L/MIL/12/92	1966311
6	1868-69	L/MIL/10/80	1867337-38	1866-67	L/MIL/11/78	1885741	1870-72	L/MIL/12/93	1966311-12
7	1869-70	L/MIL/10/81	1867338	1867-68	L/MIL/11/79	1885741	1872-74	L/MIL/12/94	1966312
8	1870	L/MIL/10/82	1867338	1868-69	L/MIL/11/80	1885816	1874-76	L/MIL/12/95	1966312-13
9	1870-71	L/MIL/10/83	1867338	1869-71	L/MIL/11/81	1885816	1876-78	L/MIL/12/96	1966313
10	1871-72	L/MIL/10/84	1867339	1871-72	L/MIL/11/82	1885817	1878-81	L/MIL/12/97	1966313
11	1872-74	L/MIL/10/85	1867339	1871-73	L/MIL/11/83	1885817	1882-83	L/MIL/12/98	1966314
12	1874-75	L/MIL/10/86	1867339-40	1873-75	L/MIL/11/84	1885818	1884-87	L/MIL/12/99	1966314
13	1875-76	L/MIL/10/87	1867340	1875-77	L/MIL/11/85	1885818	1888-89	L/MIL/12/100	1966314 and 78
14	1876-78	L/MIL/10/88	1867340	1877-78	L/MIL/11/86	1885819	1890-92	L/MIL/12/101	1966378
15	1878-79	L/MIL/10/89	1867340-41	1878-81	L/MIL/11/87	1885819			
16	1879-80	L/MIL/10/90	1867341	1882	L/MIL/11/88	1885820			
17	1880	L/MIL/10/91	1867341	1883-84	L/MIL/11/89	1885820			
18	1881	L/MIL/10/92	1867341 & 1867388	1885-88	L/MIL/11/90	1885820			
19	1882	L/MIL/10/93	1867388	1889-90	L/MIL/11/91	1885820			
20	1883	L/MIL/10/94	1867388	1891-92	L/MIL/11/92	1885820			
21	1884	L/MIL/10/95	1867388						
22	1885	L/MIL/10/96	1885473						
23	1886-87	L/MIL/10/97	1867389						
24	1888-92	L/MIL/10/98-	1867389						

Note: similar records continue from 1892 to 1916 in series L/MIL/14/1-49 which are indexed in Z/L/MIL/14/1-2. More records are also available in L/MIL/14/239 onwards.

Note: These records apply to Departmental and Warrant Officers as well as Surgeons, Assistant Surgeons and, of course, fully commissioned officers.

8.3 Officers' Casualty Returns

A further series of records, one for each presidency, covers the officers' casualties in service. In this instance, the term 'casualty' generally means the death or retirement of the officer concerned. In fact, dependent upon the presidency and the date, Departmental Officers, Warrant Officers and even Non-Commissioned Officers may be included. References are provided in:

Army Officers' Casualty Returns

	IOR Ref.	Dates	LDS Film No.
Bengal	L/MIL/10/104 to 107	1824 – 1895	1867390
Madras	L/MIL/11/93 to 95	1800 – 1853	1885828
	L/MIL/11/96 to 98	1853 – 1895	1885829
Bombay	L/MIL/12/102	1844 – 1866	1966378
	L/MIL/12/103	1852 – 1865	1966378-379
	L/MIL/12/104	1867 – 1889	1966379
	L/MIL/12/105	1889 – 1895	1966379

Note also that Officer Casualties are also published in the various Presidency Almanacs and Directories and in the Presidency and Indian Army Lists.

8.4 Officers' Military Fund Pension Contributions

An officer made contributions to his pension scheme (see Section 15) throughout his service. Records of these payments, can give a synopsis of his career, with dates of each promotion, his marriage, birth of his children, furlough in Europe and his eventual retirement and death. These records are of genealogical importance, not only because they provide details of his career progress but since they record certain details of his family, and include:

Presidency	Bengal	Madras	Bombay
IOR Ref:	L/AG/23/6/1	L/AG/23/10/1	L/AG/23/12/1-4
LDS Film No.	1866713	1850712	1850760-62
Date Range	1824-1862	1808-1862	1816-1862
Data Given	Officer's Name	Officer's Name	Officer's Name
	Date of Entry	Date of Birth or Baptism	Dates of Promotion
	Date of Birth	Dates of Promotion	Children's Birthdays
	Date of Marriage	Year of Admission	Arrival in India
	Date of Death	Year of (Re-) Marriage	Retirement Date
	Wife's Birthday	Family Reference No.	Marriage Date
	Wife's Date of Death	Date became Widower	Marriage Place
	Dates of Promotions	Date of (*)	
	Date of Retirement		

*Retirement (R), Invalid (I), Pension (P), Dismissal (D), Insanity (J), Death in Action (X)

8.5 Army Lists and Published Works

A number of publications, official and unofficial, are available describing various aspects of an officer's career. Some are available only in the India Office Records and, naturally, visits to them in the British Library will make it possible to undertake further investigative work. Some may be seen in major public libraries around the world and these include Presidency Army Lists, Presidency Almanacs and, more commonly, the East India Registers and Directories.

Presidency Army Lists

Mention is made at various places in this Guide, of the Presidency Army Lists. These may be regarded as the officers' equivalents of the soldiers' Muster Lists. They were initially compiled annually and, later, quarterly. They provided a list, in order of seniority, and with the dates of seniority, of all the officers serving – and sometimes on pension – in each presidency. It should be remarked that the India Office Records hold two sets of lists, both of which are classed 'Army Lists'. Among their various distinctions is the fact that the first are largely in manuscript (but printed for Madras after 1835) and the second are all printed. It is understood that the first set was for transmission to the Court of Directors in London. The second set was more for general reference in India. Naturally, much of the information is common to both and, indeed to that issued for public consultation in the East India Registers & Directories.

The style and detail of the Army Lists change little as the years proceed. The data contained in these lists was generally copied into the printed East India Register for the year concerned but, for reasons that can only be guessed, there are some small deviations of detail. In particular, some officers are included in one list but not in the other. For this reason, it might be helpful to consult both.

The Army Lists do include the various battalions to which each officer was allocated, whereas the East India Register does not. This makes the former more valuable, especially since, in conjunction with an indication from other sources of his unit's location, it facilitates the determination of this officer's own location, at least at the beginning of the year in question. Additionally, in many of the earlier Army Lists, details are provided of Medical Staff. These include the names, rank and allocation of not only Surgeons and Assistant Surgeons but of Apothecaries, Assistant Apothecaries and even some Hospital Stewards as well. Some of these are Anglo-Indians, although this fact is not specified and an Anglo-Indian may have a completely European name.

Army Lists - First Set

These first sets of lists may be found in:

Bengal	1781-1849	L/MIL/10/1-19	1867205-211
Madras	1759-1846	L/MIL/11/1-37	1885505-8 and 1885568-571
Bombay	1759-1855	L/MIL/12/1-17	1952297 and 1966143-146
Bombay (Duplicate Lists)		L/MIL/12/18-66	

Army Lists – Second Set

The Second Set of Army Lists are all printed and the information expanded significantly beyond that presented in the East India Register. In particular, a greater indication is given of the location of each unit. This usually makes it possible more quickly to deduce the station in which an officer is to be found, due allowance being made for any furlough, sick leave, detachment, etc. Exceptions to this are the officers who served in the Artillery. The locations of the Regiments or Battalions of both the European and Native Infantry are generally reported in both the Army Lists and East India Registers and Directories. They also usually note the location of officers of Engineering and of Sappers and Miners individually in each. This is not the case for the Artillery.

The Corps of Artillery in each Presidency was broken down into a number of Battalions (Brigades in the case of the Horse Artillery), each of which comprised an Headquarters plus four or six Companies (Troops in the case of the Horse Artillery). Each company was generally posted to widely differing stations. The station to which any particular company was posted is very difficult to identify and only appear in the Army Lists for later years. In Madras, this is as late as 1839.

It may be worthy of note that these lists include the regiments of the British Army serving in the relevant presidency. Bengal, from 1837. Madras, from 1810 and Bombay from 1856. The Bombay lists include the Indian Navy 1838 and 1848-1862 and the Hyderabad Forces in 1838 and 1848-1857. All provide War Services for British Officers in later years. (see Section 17)

This series continues well after end of the Company era. None of this series of Army Lists has been filmed by the LDS. However, they are available in the IOR as follows:

Bengal	1819 – 1889	L/MIL/17/2/1-267
Madras	1810 – 1895	L/MIL/17/3/1-329
Bombay	1823 – 1895	L/MIL/17/4/1-362

For many years these were printed quarterly rather than annually and so interpolation as a means of identifying the List for the required year is not possible.

Note that a separate source of career data for Bengal officers serving between 1795 and 1810 is available in L/MIL/17/2/268

East India Registers & Directories

These Directories were published from 1803 until 1860, but known more simply as the India Register from 1843-1860. For each Presidency, they contain a list of all the military officers serving in Staff or Regimental positions regiment by regiment. It appears evident that the publishers drew upon the data presented in the official 'Army Lists' and reproduced this for the benefit of the public at large. As indicated, there are minor discrepancies to be found and also certain less significant data were omitted.

It is understood that these directories are to be found in major libraries around the world and a small number of them are available digitised on CD.

Other Published Sources

A major reference source for *Officers of the Bengal Army, 1758 to 1834* is a four-volume work of that name comprising a compendium of officers' career histories compiled by Major V.C.P. Hodson, published by Constable & Co. between 1927 and 1947. Hodson even includes information on the origin of many officers and some details of their wills. This work is available from the LDS: Surname initial letters 'A-R' (Vols 1-3) in Film No. 2105290 Items 3-5 and 'R-Z' (Vols 3 and 4) in Film No. 2105291 Items 1-2.

It should be mentioned that Major Hodson prepared a very large number of 'cards' giving career and biographical details of the officers of the Madras and Bombay Armies and of the later Indian Army. These are available for consultation by appointment or Reader's Ticket at the National Army Museum in Chelsea, London, as are the original cards for the Bengal Army. The cards for all three armies are often updated as new information comes to light.

In addition, an alphabetical *'List of Officers of The Indian Army'* by Dodwell and Miles, was published by Longman, Orme, Brown & Co. in 1838. This work includes officers of all three Presidencies and may be viewed in LDS Films 2105289 (A to L) and 2105290 (M-Z).

Other sources of information may be found in the Presidency Government General Orders, Commander-in-Chief's General Orders (both IOR series L/MIL/17) or 'Military Proceedings' (IOR series P). One might wish to consult newspapers, military despatches or books written about the various wars, battles or other activities in which an ancestor may have taken part.

A note on officers who served in the Artillery.

For each Presidency, a book has been published which lists all the officers who served in the Artillery together with the dates of their promotion to each rank until they died or retired. These are entitled:

List of officers who have served in the regiment of the Bengal Artillery by Major-General F. W. Stubbs (Bath 1892)

A List of the officers who have served in the Madras Artillery by Major J. H. Leslie (Leicester, 1900)

The Bombay Artillery. List of officers who have served in the regiment of Bombay Artillery by Colonel F. W. M. Spring (London 1902)

Another classic publication, which summarizes many officers' careers, is:
Addiscombe: its heroes and men of note by H.M. Vibart (London 1894)

Finally, for those interested in Medical Officers, it is recommended to read D. G. Crawford's *History of the Indian Medical Service 1600-1913*, 2 vols (London 1914), and for a comprehensive list with brief biographical details of all members of the service see the same author's *Roll of the Indian Medical Service, 1615-1930* (London 1930).

9. Soldiers' Career Patterns

9.1 General

As one might expect, the great majority of soldiers (other ranks) of the Company's armies were native Indians. Indeed, the many regiments of Native Infantry comprised the largest contingents of these armies and the word 'Native' featured in their official titles. However, a number of regiments were reserved solely for European troops and such regiments generally had the word 'European' in their official titles. The limitation of admission to Europeans was strictly adhered to, maybe because the authorities were concerned about possible disaffection. Even recruits born in India and claiming to be solely of European descent were vetted to ensure that this was correct. Despite this, a limited number of 'Anglo-Indians' are believed to have served in European regiments, although maybe as Drummers or Buglers, duties for which they were readily accepted into Native regiments.

Comparisons have sometimes been made between the Company's armies and the French Foreign Legion. In the latter, a man of criminal activity could escape the law and remove himself from a society which might otherwise have deprived him of his life or liberty. Although India was far removed from England, and creditors, outraged fathers, etc. would be most unlikely to pursue any miscreant there, the Company endeavoured to recruit soldiers of higher quality. Indeed, given particularly the opportunities for advancement to positions within and beyond the army in Britain's rapidly expanding interests in India, the Company attracted some middle class men who, possibly caught up in hard times at home, were also seeking a stable career with good pay, three square meals a day and a pension upon their retirement. Thus, although the soldiers included a number of habitual drunkards, ne'er-do-wells, and even some time re-captured deserters from the British Army, the characteristics of the average HEIC soldier were generally of a higher level than those of 'the scum-of-the-earth' as Wellington described the average soldier of the British Army. In the mid and late eighteenth century, a number of Protestant 'Swiss' mercenaries were engaged, as were Europeans of a variety of other origins. Many were 'soldiers of fortune' who had previously been recruited by the armies of other nations, but who, for a variety of reasons, had wished to transfer to the English East India Company. Such included Dutchmen, Danes and even Frenchmen. Furthermore, to augment the forces in India at the time of the second Mysore War, King George III, as Elector of Hanover, was prevailed upon to despatch two Hanoverian regiments to Madras. A number of these soldiers later transferred to the Madras Army.

A man was generally recruited into either the Infantry or the Artillery right from the start. Generally, all that was seemingly necessary was that he was in good health, aged at least 19 years and not on the 'run' either from the law or from the King's service. Large numbers of recruits falsely claimed to be 19 years of age. There was originally a minimum height regulation but this was systematically reduced as recruitment became more difficult at the time of the Napoleonic Wars. Nevertheless many were still found to have placed cardboard in their shoes to achieve the required standard! Following approval on grounds of health and general suitability, the recruit 'Attested' that he was willing to serve in the Company's Army and that he accepted the disciplines imposed under the 'Articles of War'. Copies of these attestations are extremely rare, unlike similar ones in the British Army.

Prior to 1796, most recruits were required to sign up for 5 years service but from that date, it was increased to 10 years, in line with recruits to the King's Army. Shortly afterwards, the Company accepted recruits for 'Unlimited Service' but this latter was frequently for deserters from the King's Army, for whom the alternative was imprisonment. In 1806 the regulations were changed and options between seven years and 'Unlimited Service' were available. From 1812, the options were reduced either to twelve years or 'Unlimited Service', which in India, meant eighteen years with an option to extend. The great majority then accepted 'Unlimited Service' although twelve years became more common in the 1840s and 1850s.

The recruit was sent to the Company's Reception Depôt to await embarkation for India. For some men this waiting time was only two or three weeks. Men recruited in later years as Sappers remained in England for about a year to be specially trained alongside their opposite numbers in the Royal Engineers. In exceptional circumstances a recruit could wait as long as two years before embarkation for India! Much depended upon the date of recruitment and the scheduling of the ship nominated to take him to his allotted presidency. The sailing 'season' commenced on the first of January. Ships destined for Bengal generally sailed in January to June. Ships for Madras most frequently sailed in March to May and those for Bombay sailed at any time in the first six months of the year. The voyages tended to take a fairly consistent four months and the dates of sailing were largely determined by the state of prevailing winds and sea at the appropriate points in the voyage and at their destination. Rather few ships sailed from England later than the end of June each year.

It is important to note that the name of the ship and year of the man's arrival in India stayed alongside a soldier's name throughout his service. This was to assist identification of the correct man among many of the same forename-surname combination. Additionally, each corps in each Presidency allocated a sequence number to each soldier upon arrival. This sequence number becomes evident in the 'Muster Lists' taken annually, although was subject to some changes and so can not be wholly relied upon..

Upon arrival in India, the soldier would have been sent to the headquarters company of the regiment to which he was allocated. Beware, there are a number of examples of his being sent to a different service from that to which he may have been recruited. For example, if he had been recruited as an infantryman and the presidency army was short of artillerymen, he could have been selected to transfer to the artillery. Furthermore, certain artillerymen were selected to serve in the Horse Artillery and, until they were specially recruited as such in the 1840's, others were selected to become Pioneers or Sappers and Miners. Following this initial training, the soldier would be sent on the 'march', maybe several hundred miles, to join his new colleagues already posted to his regiment/company wherever in the presidency they might be stationed. Evidently, such marches would include several men, plus any wives and children, properly led by an officer and accompanied by other experienced soldiers.

The soldier is subsequently listed in the 'Muster List' for his regiment, generally taken on 1st January every year. His rank is reported in these muster lists and so any increase in rank can be noted as having taken place at some time in the previous year. Occasionally, he may have been transferred from one regiment or battalion to another. In such a case, he should appear in the 'Casualty Roll' of his former regiment. It is important to remember that a 'Casualty' is a man's removal from his regiment for any reason whatever. This may be any reason from a simple transfer to his death. The current meanings of casualty as severe wounding or death are only two of the many meanings of earlier days. Of course, in addition, if he took part in any campaign, he might be listed in returns of those entitled to a medal or to 'prize money'.

A man might spend the whole of his career, possibly the full 18 years, with the same regiment. He might then be offered the opportunity to extend his service by a further three years with the promise of an enhanced pension at the end. Some soldiers then even accepted yet another three years service, again for an increased pension. They might then retire, either remaining in India, returning home or, going to live in one of Britain's colonies around the world.

Some soldiers, having spent about seven to ten years with a 'front line' regiment, were invited to be promoted to the rank of Corporal and to transfer to the 'Town Major's List' (called 'Effective Supernumeraries' in Madras Presidency). This 'list' provided support services such as laboratory, supplies and ordnance, or to partake in the duties of the 'Department of Public Works' (DPW) which was responsible for roads, bridges, irrigation, etc. Such soldiers would be mustered annually in the 'Town Major's List'. A man could be promoted within the Town Major's List to Serjeant, Serjeant-Major, Sub-Conductor and then to Conductor. These two latter ranks were termed 'Warrant Officers' and from the latter rank a small number of men were further promoted to the ranks of 'Honorary Lieutenant', 'Honorary Captain', 'Honorary Major' or even 'Honorary Lieutenant-Colonel'.

A number of married men were recruited and they were permitted to take their wives, plus any children, to India with them. In the mid-1820s married men appear to have represented six percent of soldiers embarking. Other soldiers married whilst in India. In the late 18th and early 19th century, and with the great scarcity of European girls in those years, the soldier would often find a wife from among the local Indian population whom he would almost certainly have to convert to Christianity. This led, naturally, to the growth of an 'Anglo-Indian' population. Other soldiers would choose a wife who was the daughter or widow of a colleague, or who was one of the girls of the 'Orphan Asylum'. Provision was made for soldiers' legitimate daughters in the form of an allowance to their fathers until they were aged 14 years, at which time it ceased (see page 47). The local Bishop recognized this and readily granted licences for girls of this age to get married. This largely accounts for the significant number of marriages in which the bride was only 14 years of age.

A soldier was permitted in his spare time to practise for profit a particular skill that he may have acquired before enlisting in the army. Thus, a joiner, for example, could make furniture for sale to his colleagues. There was generally a supply of native labour on hand to undertake the less exacting tasks and a company would employ these to do their washing, cut their hair, etc.

At the end of his contracted period of service, the soldier and his wife were sent back to his previous residence in Europe. A large number opted to remain in India, either as Veterans or simply as Pensioners, with the permission of the Company.

9.2 A Note on Roman Catholics

In the early days of the Company's armies there had been discrimination against the recruitment of Roman Catholics. Indeed, rather than accept them, even in times of poor response to their recruiting efforts, the Company recruited soldiers from Protestant 'Swiss Mercenaries'. However, with the onset of conflict with France and her allies, following their Revolution, this source of recruits was effectively cut off. In addition at the same time, the King required to expand his own armies to counter the French threat and the Company found itself in direct conflict with him for the service of Britain's young men. Eventually, a compromise was concluded by which the Company was allocated a quota of about 2000 recruits annually for which they had to re-apply each year.

Although no formal rescinding of their policy has been reported, both the King and the Company were forced to recruit in Ireland and to accept Roman Catholics into their services. The number of Catholics rose steadily in the early 19th century to as many as fifty percent of the Company's recruits by the late 1820's. The Catholic Emancipation Act was passed by Parliament in Westminster in 1829 and its effect was felt in India shortly thereafter. The Company not only modified its practices to acknowledge the large number of Catholics in its service, but paid for chaplains for them and, soon afterwards, contributed funds for the construction of chapels and churches for them in its major stations.

9.3 A Note on Anglo-Indians

In the late 18th century, the Company shipped thousands of soldiers to India but few, if any, women were permitted to accompany them. A policy was introduced which promoted marriage of these soldiers with native women, indeed a bounty was paid to men so marrying. The proviso was that the native women converted to Christianity and this was seen as a modest start to the Christianization of India. Naturally, this resulted in the birth of many children of mixed race variously termed 'Indo-Britons', 'Eurasians', or, preferably today, 'Anglo-Indians'.

Anglo-Indian boys were frequently anxious to follow their fathers' careers and to join the army. They were not permitted to join European Regiments unless they were ethnically totally European. Thus, many of them opted to serve in positions in the native regiments and, very commonly, as bandsmen. Frequently also, they are found to have been appointed as 'Hospital Stewards' or 'Assistant Apothecaries' in the 'Indian Subordinate Medical Service'. Although these men are rarely named in the 'Muster Lists', mention is made of them in the various sets of the Army Lists from 1819 (Bengal), 1829 (Madras) and 1832 (Bombay). Further, they can be found in the Directories of Bengal (from 1815) and Bombay (from 1832). They only appear in the Madras Directories after 1862.

There are, of course some notable exceptions to this. Such is the case, for example, of Lieutenant-Colonel James Skinner (1778-1841) of the celebrated Skinner's Horse, founded as an irregular cavalry unit in 1803. Skinner was the son of Lieutenant-Colonel Hercules Skinner and a Rajput lady.

10. Recruitment of Soldiers

10.1 Recruitment Records

Soldiers were recruited in much the same way as to the army of the Crown. Recruiting parties were initially based at offices in London, then later in Liverpool and Bristol in England, Glasgow in Scotland and, later still, Dublin, Cork and Newry in Ireland. Experienced soldiers were sent around the country to convince the young men with whom they came into contact, of the good life with a secure income that they could lead in the Company's armies in India and that they could retire on an attractive pension for the rest of their lives. Recruits were given the 'Company's Shilling' and sent to the "Depôt" to await shipment to India. These men were eligible to serve either in the Artillery, the Infantry or, later, in the 'Sappers and Miners'. Later still, a number were recruited for service in the Cavalry. Men above about 5ft 7 ins. were generally assigned to the Artillery and those below to the Infantry. Exceptions to this may be found, particularly in the earlier years.

Recruitment Lists are available for both Artillery and Infantry from the following dates:

For recruits in:	London	1817	Dublin	1843
	Liverpool	1825	Newry	1846
	Bristol	1846	Cork	1846
	North Britain (Scotland)	1819		

Note that men were recruited from these places well before these dates but no records giving the particulars of such recruitment survive. Full details of the IOR References and Film Numbers are given on the next page, together with an example of data typically found for an individual soldier.

It should be noted that recruits were also subject to checks of health, height and age. Such checks were lacking in rigour, however, notably that on a recruit's age! More importantly, verification was required that they were not 'on the run', particularly from the Law or from service with the forces of the Crown.

Early recruits were mustered on the Isle of Wight for transport in the Company's ships to India. A formal Depôt for the recruits awaiting shipment was established at Newport on the Isle of Wight in 1801 and then replaced by a newer and larger Depôt (Brompton Barracks) at Chatham in Kent in 1811. Finally, in 1843 the Depôt was transferred to Warley in Essex and remained there until the end of the Company era.

Registers of Recruits to the East India Company's Armies

IOR Ref:	LDS Film	Dates	Recruiting Centre
L/MIL/9/1	1786428	1817 - 1819	London
L/MIL/9/2	1786428	1819 - Feb 1822	London
L/MIL/9/3	1786428	Oct 1825-Jan 1829	London
L/MIL/9/4	1786428	Feb 1829-Dec 1834	London
L/MIL/9/5	1786428	Jan 1835-May 1840	London
L/MIL/9/6	1786428-29	May 1840-Aug 1843	London
L/MIL/9/7	1786429	Sep 1843-May 1853	London
L/MIL/9/8	1786429	May 1853-Jul 1860	London
L/MIL/9/9	1786429	Sep 1827-Dec 1840	Liverpool
L/MIL/9/10	1786430	Jan 1841-Jun 1857	Liverpool
L/MIL/9/11	1786430	Jun 1857-Jul 1859	Liverpool
L/MIL/9/12	1786430	Nov 1857-Jul 1860	Liverpool - Cavalry Only
L/MIL/9/13	1786430	May 1846-Nov 1850	Bristol
L/MIL/9/14	1786430	Nov 1850-May 1856	Bristol
L/MIL/9/15	1786430	May 1856-Apr 1859	Bristol
L/MIL/9/16	1786430	Mar 1859-Jul 1860	Bristol
L/MIL/9/17	1786430	Jul 1819-Aug 1824	North Britain
L/MIL/9/18	1786430	Aug 1824-May 1827	North Britain
L/MIL/9/19	1786431	May 1839-Aug 1851	North Britain
L/MIL/9/20	1786431	Oct 1851-Mar 1858	North Britain
L/MIL/9/21	1786431	Mar 1858-Jul 1860	North Britain
L/MIL/9/22	1786431	Jan 1843-Jul 1855	Dublin
L/MIL/9/23	1786431	Jul 1855-Dec 1858	Dublin
L/MIL/9/24	1786431	Dec 1858-Jul 1860	Dublin
L/MIL/9/25	1786483	May 1846-Dec 1857	Newry
L/MIL/9/26	1786483	Jan 1858-Jul 1860	Newry
L/MIL/9/27	1786483	Jan 1846-Nov 1851	Cork
L/MIL/9/28	1786483	Nov 1851-Jul 1860	Cork

Example of Entry in a Recruit Register

L/MIL/9/9 – Register of Recruits Liverpool September 1827 – December 1840

Artillery/Infantry:	Infantry	Date of Enlistment:	3rd October 1828
Name:	Edward Evans	Date of Attestation:	6th
Age:	19	Intermediate Approval:	11th
Size:	5 ft. 5 ¼ ins.	Final Approval:	23rd
Complexion:	Fresh	Period of Service:	Unlimited
Eyes:	Hazle (sic)	Trade or Profession:	Silversmith
Hair:	D. Brown	Married or Single:	Single
Born – Parish:	Greenwich	Where enlisted:	Manchester
County	Kent	Remarks:	Embarked 16th Oct
Kingdom	England	Enlisting Serjeant:	Shaw

10.2 Depôt Description Lists

Roughly from the beginning of the nineteenth century, the Company established 'Depôt Description Lists', sometimes referred to as 'Depôt Lists'. These gave details of each recruit, generally very similar to those in the Recruitment Register, plus a limited amount extra. The lists are ordered by Name of the Ship in order of its date of sailing for India. The detailed references to the Depôt Lists are given below.

Depôt Description Lists

IOR Ref:	Dates Covered	Service	Depôt	LDS Film
L/MIL/9/29	Jul 1811 – Dec 1819	Artillery	Chatham	1786483
L/MIL/9/30	Jan 1820 – Dec 1830	Artillery	Chatham	1786483
L/MIL/9/31	Jan 1831 – Dec 1838	Artillery	Chatham	1786484
L/MIL/9/32	Jan 1839 – Dec 1846	Artillery	Chatham/Warley	1786484
L/MIL/9/33	Jan 1847 – Jul 1855	Artillery	Warley	1786484
L/MIL/9/34	Jul 1855 – Jul 1860	Artillery	Warley	1786485
L/MIL/9/35	Oct 1857 – Dec 1859	Cavalry	Warley	1786485
L/MIL/9/36	Jan 1860 – Jul 1860	Cavalry	Warley	1786485
L/MIL/9/37*	1801 – 1815	Infantry	Newport I. O. W.	1786485/6
L/MIL/9/38**	1801 – 1809	Infantry	Newport I. O. W.	1785486
L/MIL/9/39***	1806 – 1809	Infantry	Newport I. O. W.	1785486
L/MIL/9/40	Sep 1810 – Jun 1815	Infantry	Newport I. O. W.	1785486
L/MIL/9/41	Jan 1816 – Dec 1826	Infantry	Chatham	1785486/7
L/MIL/9/42	Jan 1827 – Jun 1839	Infantry	Chatham	1785487
L/MIL/9/43	Jul 1839 – Dec 1845	Infantry	Chatham/Warley	1785487
L/MIL/9/44	Jan 1846 – Dec 1853	Infantry	Warley	1866879
L/MIL/9/45	Jan 1854 – Jul 1860	Infantry	Warley	1785487/8

*Includes lists of recruits sent to India 1802-15 and those embarked by ship 1805-11
** Description Books Aug 1802-Feb 1806 and Embarkations by ship 1801 – 1809
*** Description Books Aug 1806-Jun 1809 and Deserters from Prison Ships 1805-09

An Example of an Entry in such a Depôt List (L/MIL/9/42) is:

Ship:	'Thames'	**Born – Parish**	Greenwich
Date of Embarkation:	6 March 1829	**County**	Kent
Presidency:	Madras	**Kingdom**	England
Corps:	Infantry	**By whom &**	Axford
Name:	Edward Evans	**Where enlisted:**	Manchester
Age:	19	**When joined Depôt:**	22 October 1828
Height:	5 ft. 5 ¼ ins.	**Date of Enlistment &**	3 October
Visage:	Long	**Attestation:**	6 October
Hair:	D. Brown	**Period of Service**	Unlimited
Eyes:	Hazle (sic)	**Remarks:**	-----
Complexion:	Fresh		

10.3 Embarkation Lists

Embarkation was effected at the Isle of Wight until the Depôt moved to Chatham in 1815. Then it was from Gravesend towards the Thames Estuary. A fresh list was drawn up as each group of soldiers left the Depôt and was embarked aboard the ship in which they were selected to travel to India. These lists, referred to as 'Embarkation Lists' are available by date of sailing. In fact, they date from as early as 1740 and represent some of the earliest lists of recruits available.

These 'Embarkation Lists' are available in three groups:

- The first group (L/MIL/9/85 – 102) extends from 1740 to 1854
- The second group (L/MIL/9/77 – 82) extends from 1824 to 1860
- The third group (L/MIL/9/83) extends from February 1819 to October 1840
  (Note that this third group is simply a list of soldiers embarked in each ship)

Evidently, a number of the 'Embarkation Lists' feature in both major series but, strangely, the lists are not identical in terms of the data supplied for each recruit. This means that it is worthwhile to examine both series.   The next two pages offer a list giving the precise references to be consulted followed by an example of the data provided in each list for a particular recruit in a particular ship. The information provided in the 'Embarkation Lists' generally increases with the date. For the earliest dates, for example, L/MIL/9/85

List of 35 Soldiers on board the ship 'King William' Captain James Sanders Commander for Fort St. George.

Published at East India House, 7 February 1740

Name	Quality	County	Trade	Age
James Garvay	Soldier	Ireland	Labourer	20
Henry Chambers	Soldier	London	Painter	25
James Phipps	Soldier	Wiltshire	Woolstapler	27
Etc.				

These data may be compared with those provided in later years in the examples given below.

Note that in later years wives and children are recorded with their husbands. At least from the middle 1820s, the Company seems to have recruited a fairly constant six percent married men and not only permitted them to take their wives, but gave them an allowance during their husband's service and eventually a pension, if they survived him. Any children were also permitted to accompany their parents and their father was granted additional allowances for them until they reached the age of fourteen.

Note also that recruitment and service details may sometimes be found in papers relating to admissions to pension. This is further discussed in Section 16.1.

Again, some soldiers, who were recruited towards the end of the Company period, feature in the 'snapshot' of pensioners taken in 1896. These provide recruitment and service details and may be found in L/MIL/14/214 and 215 (No LDS Film available).

Records of Embarkation Lists

First Series

IOR References	Dates Covered	LDS Film
L/MIL/9/85	1740 – 1763	1835456
L/MIL/9/86	Oct 1767 – Mar 1769	1835456
L/MIL/9/87	Sep 1769 – Apr 1772	1835457
L/MIL/9/88	Oct 1772 – May 1778	1835457
L/MIL/9/89	Jan 1774 – 1778	1835457
L/MIL/9/90	Jan 1775 – Dec 1784	1835457
L/MIL/9/91	Jan 1784 – Apr 1787	1835457
L/MIL/9/92	Oct 1787 – Apr 1788	1835457
L/MIL/9/93	Nov 1789 – Apr 1791	1835458
L/MIL/9/94	Nov 1791 – Apr 1792	1835458
L/MIL/9/95	Nov 1792 – May 1794	1835458
L/MIL/9/96	Jan 1792 – Dec 1797	1835458
L/MIL/9/97	Dec 1799 – Dec 1809	1835458
L/MIL/9/98	Jan 1810 – Feb 1816	1835691
L/MIL/9/99	Mar 1816 – Jun 1824	1866880
L/MIL/9/100	Jan 1825 – Dec 1839	1835691
L/MIL/9/101	Feb 1840 – Nov 1847	1835691
L/MIL/9/102	Mar 1848 – Aug 1854	1835691

Second Series

IOR References	Dates Covered	LDS Film
L/MIL/9/77	Jan 1824 – Oct 1832	1835455
L/MIL/9/78	Jan 1833 – Nov 1843	1835455
L/MIL/9/79	Feb 1844 – Oct 1849	1866705
L/MIL/9/80	Mar 1850 – Nov 1855	1866705
L/MIL/9/81	Jun 1856 – Nov 1858	1835456
L/MIL/9/82	Jan 1859 – Jul 1860	1835456

Note that each reference contains a list of troopships in order of their date of sailing for India. For each ship is given the name of her commander, date of sailing, destination and a list of recruits embarked with details of each as given below. At the end of the list, a tally is given of the number of recruits for each service (Artillery or Infantry) and numbers of women and children, plus the date and place of arrival.

Example of Data in 'Embarkation Lists'

Return of Military Embarked on The Honourable Company's Ship "Minerva"
For Madras, George Probyn Esq., Commander. Chatham, 12th May 1827
(Landed at Madras 24th August 1827)

(There follows a list of 250 recruits, including the data shown below on each. The data are written in a series of rows, one row for each soldier. However, for simplicity the example below is transcribed vertically. As indicated, for the period 1824 to 1854, two series of entries were made).

	L/MIL/9/77	L/MIL/9/100
Corps:	Artillery	Artillery
Name:	Peter Evers	Peter Evers
Rank:	Soldier	
Age:	22	22
Height:	5 ft. 7 ½ ins.	
Parish:	Drogheda, Louth	Drogheda, Louth
Date of Enlistment:	1st January 1827	
Where Enlisted:	Drogheda	Drogheda
Date of Attestation:		1st January 1827
Period of Service:	Unlimited	
Occupation:	Weaver	Weaver
Remarks:	Wife Mary Child, Mary, 5 months	Wife Mary 22 Mary 6 months
Landed at Madras	24th August 1827	
Recapitulation:	Men 250 Women 15 Children 7	

Note that the child Mary was 5 or 6 months old at the time of sailing on 12th May 1827. This was only 5 months after Peter Evers enlisted on 1st January that year and so the Recruiting Officer was evidently prepared to accept this recruit with his wife plus a very new-born child.

10.4 Ships' Logs

Further records are available in the form of Ships' Logs, referred to as 'Journals'. These Journals were to be deposited with the Company records upon completion of each voyage. Unfortunately, they cease in the mid-1830s when the Company stopped using its own vessels but contracted out the troop carrying function to others. Although these documents do not generally provide additional genealogical data they may yield some interesting background. Researchers may therefore wish to inspect the Captain's Log of the ship carrying their ancestor to India. These are available in the IOR Series L/MAR/. A reference book on the IOR Reading Room open shelves lists, in date order, the name of the ship and its destinations en route to the East and back to England. These records have not been filmed by the LDS. For example, Reference: L/MAR/14 R

Journal of the Proceedings on Board the Honourable East India Company Ship 'Minerva' from Port of London to Madras, Penang, China, Madras, St. Helena & back to London, commencing 10th May 1827.   Commander: George Probyn.

L/MAR/14 R then provides lists of:

- The Ship's Company, with rank etc.
- The Private Passengers
- The King's Officers and Soldiers embarked for Madras
- The Honourable Company Recruits for Madras

This latter gives the following information about each recruit:

No.:	94
Name:	Peter Evers
Description:	Private, Artillery
Where & when received on board:	12th May 1827, Gravesend
Where & when landed:	24th August 1827, Madras
Women:	Mary Evers, wife of Private Peter Evers
Children:	Mary Evers, aged 6 months

The ships' logs make most interesting reading. Not only do they record the weather and ships' positions daily, and the amount of drinking water remaining each Sunday, but births and deaths occurring and any disciplinary matters. If you are lucky (!), your ancestor may be singled out for mention. For example:

Tuesday, 12th June 1827 – Soldiers employed picking oakum.
A.M. Ordered Court of Enquiry on the conduct of Privates Hugh McNally and John Messenger, the former for repeated absence from his musters, the latter for striking a sentry
Latitude 8 deg. 02 N. Longitude 18 deg. 58 W.

Wednesday, 13th June 1827- Punished Hugh McNally with two dozen lashes and John Messenger with three dozen lashes by sentence of the Court of Enquiry.   Sick: Seamen – 4, Troops – 23.
Latitude 7 deg. 37 N. Longitude 18 deg. 51 W.

11. Soldiers' Services

11.1 Soldiers' Records

For the period 1772-1798 service details can sometimes be found in a soldier's pension papers. See section 16.1.

From 1831, a summary record was kept of the service of each soldier who was still living and serving at that date, or who joined after that date. In other words, soldiers who had died or retired prior to that date were not included. These records, referred to as 'Registers of European Soldiers', provide a very brief but useful synopsis of a soldier's details and career. They probably represent the best starting point for researchers who may only know that their ancestor served as a soldier in the Company's army and was still alive in 1831.

The references are given in detail on the next page, following an example of the data, which are typically contained in them. Frequently, several questions remain unanswered but, crucially for those starting out, they almost always include the Town and County of origin of the soldier plus the name of the ship bringing him and year of his arrival in India.

Example from Soldiers' Records of Service

An example from L/MIL/11/101 (Madras) of details that may be found in these records. Note that some data are not always provided. Also, since this soldier transferred to the India Army's 'Unattached List' in 1861, the last two headings remain uncompleted.

Presidency:	Madras
Entered Service:	1829
Name:	Edward Evans
Rank or Situation:	Gunner, 3d. Battalion, Artillery
Occupation before Enlisting:	Silversmith
Town & County:	Greenwich, Kent
Date of Attestation:	(Left Blank)
Where Enlisted:	(Left Blank)
Form of Contracted Service:	Unlimited
On what ship arrive from Europe:	'Thames'
Remarks:	Transferred Effective Supernumeraries, 1st Decr. 1837
	Laby. Man. Serjeant Instructor, 1841,Sub-Conductor, Feb. 1852
Date & Nature of Casualty:	(Left blank)
Amount of Estate and how disposed of:	(Left Blank)

In section 8.2 we described details of summary service records compiled for officers who were granted furlough in Europe between 1859 and 1873. In fact, they also include a limited number of Departmental and Warrant Officers and senior N.C.O.s, who successfully applied for leave of absence in Europe. Thus, if you have Departmental, Warrant Officers or senior N.C.O.s in your family, also make reference to section 8.2.

Registers of European Soldiers' Services

(for those still serving in 1831 and those recruited up to 1860)

For soldiers recruited	Surnames	Bengal		Madras		Bombay	
		IOR Ref.	LDS Film	IOR Ref.	LDS Film	IOR Ref.	LDS Film
1793 – 1839	A – K	L/MIL/10/122	1867444	L/MIL/11/101	1885890	L/MIL/12/109	1966380
1793 – 1839	L – N	L/MIL/10/123	1867444	L/MIL/11/102	1885890	L/MIL/12/110	1966380
1793 – 1839	N - P	L/MIL/10/123	1867445	L/MIL/11/102	1885890	L/MIL/12/110	1966380
1793 – 1839	P – Z	L/MIL/10/123	1867445	L/MIL/11/102	1885890	L/MIL/12/110	1966381
1840 – 1850	A – H	L/MIL/10/124	1885473	L/MIL/11/103	1885891	L/MIL/12/111	1966381
1840 – 1850	I – K	L/MIL/10/124	1885474	L/MIL/11/103	1885891	L/MIL/12/111	1966381
1840 – 1850	L – W	L/MIL/10/125	1885474	L/MIL/11/104	1885891	L/MIL/12/112	1966381
1840 – 1850	W – Z	L/MIL/10/125	1885474	L/MIL/11/104	1885891	L/MIL/12/112	1966382
1851 – 1857	A – K	L/MIL/10/126	1867445	L/MIL/11/105	1885892	L/MIL/12/113	1966382
1851 – 1857	L – Z	L/MIL/10/127	1867446	L/MIL/11/106	1885892	L/MIL/12/114	1966382
1858 – 1860	A – K	L/MIL/10/128	1867446	L/MIL/11/107	1885892	L/MIL/12/115	1966382
1858 – 1860	L – Z	L/MIL/10/129	1867447	L/MIL/11/108	1885892	L/MIL/12/116	1966382

Note: If you have come to learn that an ancestor served as a soldier in one of the East India Company's Armies, it is suggested that these are the first records to view and to use them to determine the name of the ship bringing him to India and the date of its arrival. Beware, however, there may be a number of soldiers with the same name!

11.2 Muster Rolls

This section is entitled 'Muster Rolls' but is used to include a description of 'Nominal Rolls', sometimes 'Casualty Rolls' and even, in the case of Bombay, simple 'Inventories and Effects Records' of deceased soldiers.

Probably, the most frequently consulted surviving records for Warrant Officers, Non-Commissioned Officers and Rank and File are the Annual Muster Rolls. The inclusion of Warrant Officers (Conductors and Sub-Conductors) was sporadic prior to 1861. In Madras, Sub-Conductors feature from 1820 to 1830. In Bombay, both Conductors and Sub-Conductors feature from 1812 to 1834. In Bengal, with very few individual exceptions, neither appears in the Muster Rolls before 1861. However, both may generally be found in the presidency Army Lists from the early nineteenth century. Some Muster Rolls, particularly in the 18th century, also include details of regimental officers.

A muster of European soldiers was taken in each Presidency on the first of January of each year and, occasionally, more frequently. The styles from each presidency vary somewhat, and also contain more information as the years progress, but much of the basic data are the same in each. In particular, the data provided by the Bombay Presidency are more copious and so more interesting than those of other presidencies. Hence our examples, given on page 45, are from Bombay.

The lists of soldiers are generally in alphabetical order by initial letter of surname and the Muster is broken down into Corps, the Corps being:

Town Major's List. (known in the Madras Presidency as list of 'Effective Supernumeraries'). This was a corps of soldiers either posted to duty as N.C.O.s in the Native Cavalry or Infantry regiments, or in a series of support roles for the army in general. Such duties were varied and a list of the titles is given in the Glossary at the end of this Guide. Most common, however, were those of Ordnance and Civil Works support. Others tend to be more directly administrative. A number of junior soldiers were also recruited directly to the Town Major's List. Most, however, were drawn from the 'front line' troops after they had served and proved themselves over about seven years.

European Artillery. For each Presidency, the Corps of Artillery was divided into Horse Artillery and European Foot Artillery. The Horse Artillery was introduced in 1805 and so does not feature before this date. Those European N.C.O.s serving with the Native Regiment of Artillery in each Presidency are listed under the particular native battalion in each presidency, known as the 'Golundauze'.

Depending upon the date of the muster, either the whole corps is mustered together, in which case the man's battalion is marked alongside his name, or it is broken down into separate battalions. Within either list, each soldier is listed in order of the initial letter of his surname. It is unfortunate that no indication of his company is given in addition. This is regrettable since all companies were generally stationed in different locations and, therefore, a knowledge of the location of an individual soldier at a particular time can be unusually difficult to obtain.

<u>Infantry</u>. Each soldier is listed in surname first letter alphabetical order regiment by regiment. For some periods of years the European Infantry was combined into a single regiment, sometimes with two 'wings'. Generally, however, it was divided into two or three individual regiments. They were not broken down into Companies in the Muster Lists and so it is difficult to impossible to determine in which company a man served.

<u>Veterans</u> and/or Invalids. Note that these two terms were frequently interchangeable. A number of soldiers who had achieved the end of their contracted service were retained as an effective reserve and formed into battalions either of Artillery or Infantry. These battalions might include soldiers who had been wounded sufficiently for them to have to withdraw from the major fighting units but not sufficiently for them to be retained in the Invalid Battalion. Again, in the Muster List each soldier is listed as for the European Infantry above.

<u>Sappers and Miners</u>   Once more, each soldier is listed as for the European Infantry above. Sappers and Miners may be compared to 'Pioneers' in the earlier days.

In all the above categories, against each man's name and surname are given his Regimental Number, Rank, Age (at date of register), Town, County and Country of Birth, Name of the Ship which brought him and the Year of his Arrival, the length of Service for which he signed up and, if appropriate, the Date at which he last re-enlisted.

Each soldier was given a Regimental Number. Of course, this was to facilitate identification. At least on one occasion, this numbering system was re-established. Furthermore, a fresh number was sometimes allocated when a man re-enlisted. So, care is advised in their use.

These Muster Lists are extensive and stretch from:

Presidency	Range	IOR References	LDS Film Nos.
Bengal – Annual	1716 - 1861	L/MIL/10/130-185	*1867447-1885423
Bengal – Quarterly	1855 - 1859	L/MIL/10/193-200	Believed unfilmed
Bengal – Deaths	1800 - 1865	L/MIL/10/186-192	*1885423-1885472
Madras – Annual	1762 - 1861	L/MIL/11/109-169	*1885893-1886055
Madras – Quarterly	1856 - 1862	L/MIL/11/170-185	*1886055-1886057
Bombay – Annual	1708 - 1865	L/MIL/12/117-197	*1966429-2029664
Bombay – Monthly	1855 - 1860	L/MIL/12/198-208	*2029666-2029727

* Beware, these LDS film numbers are not continuous and interpolation is not possible. The lists are extensive and so not reproduced here. As earlier advised, the complete list of LDS Film Numbers can be seen by inserting one of the above from the relevant presidency into the Film/Fiche search function on the LDS Family History Library Catalogue. The following does, however, give an example of what may be found in the typical Muster List for an average soldier.

Example from Soldiers' Annual Muster Rolls

Examples of the information to be found in Bombay Muster Rolls of 1800 and 1846.

L/MIL/12/136	L/MIL/12/177
An Alphabetical Roll of NCO's, Drummers & Matrosses in the Battalion of Artillery on the Bombay Establishment As they stood at 30th April, 1800	**Alphabetical Muster Roll of the European NCO's, Farriers and Trumpeters of the Honorable Company's Horse Brigade on the Bombay Establishment under the command of Lt.-Col. M.C. Decluzeau as they stood on the 30th September 1846**

Letter:	1	
Regimental No.		106
Rank:	Matross	Sergeant
Name	Aikinhead, John	Armstrong, William
Age at Date of Register	33	37
Born – Parish:		
- County		Dublin
- Country	England	Ireland
Arrived - Ship	'Duke of Montrose'	'Herefordshire'
- Date:	7 August	14 May 1829
- Year	1785	
When Re-enlisted:	9 December 1795	11 August 1845
For How long:	5 years	3 years
Service		Unlimited
From whence received		Foot Artillery

--ooOOoo--

After each list of each corps there follows a list of 'Casualties' from that corps during the preceding year. It must be remarked that 'Casualty' means a soldier removed from his corps for any reason. This may be any reason from death to promotion or simple transfer to another corps. The information given is essentially the same as for the main muster for the preceding year, plus the brief reason for the soldier becoming a 'Casualty'.

Soldiers Casualty Returns

Presidency	IOR Reference	Year of Casualty	LDS Film No.
Bengal	L/MIL/10/186	1800 – 1826	1885423
	L/MIL/10/187	1854 – 1855	1885424
	L/MIL/10/188	1856 – 1858	1885424-425
	L/MIL/10/189	1858 – 1859	1885425-470
	L/MIL/10/190-191	1859 – 1863	1885471
	L/MIL/10/192	1860 – 1865	1885472
	L/MIL/10/253-300	1866 – 1907	Unfilmed

Presidency	IOR Reference	Year of Casualty	LDS Film No.
Madras	L/MIL/11/232	1853 – 1863	1886083
	L/MIL/11/233 to 236	1862 – 1867	1886084
	L/MIL/11/237 to 242	1868 – 1873	1886121
	L/MIL/11/243 to 252	1874 – 1883	1886122
	L/MIL/11/253 to 273	1884 – 1904	1886123
	L/MIL/11/274 to 276	1905 – 1907	1886124
Bombay	L/MIL/12/198 to 199	1855 – 1856	2029666
	L/MIL/12/200 to 202	1856 – 1857	2029667
	L/MIL/12/203 to 205	1858 – 1859	2029726
	L/MIL/12/206 to 209	1859 – 1860	2029727
	L/MIL/12/210 to 215	1860 – 1862	2029728
	L/MIL/12/216	1861 – 1862	2029729
	L/MIL/12/217	1862 – 1863	2029730
	L/MIL/12/218 to 221	1862 – 1864	2029731
	L/MIL/12/222 to 224	1865 – 1866	2029732
	L/MIL/12/225 to 230	1867 – 1872	2029733
	L/MIL/12/231 to 237	1873 – 1880	2029734
	L/MIL/12/238 to 244	1880 – 1886	2029735
	L/MIL/12/245 to 255	1887 – 1897	2029778
	L/MIL/12/256 to 265	1898 – 1907	2029779

Casualty Returns are generally attached to the Annual, Quarterly or Monthly Muster Rolls. However, in the case of Bengal, these particular lists refer specifically to 'Casualties by Death'

A third list gives 'Casualties by Death' during the preceding year. Once more, this gives the same data as for the main muster for the preceding year but, additionally, details of the disposal of his estate. If he had been married, this would generally be to his widow, who is sometimes named. If he remained unmarried, the effects could be left to a regimental colleague or even to his mother or other close relative in Britain. This latter can, naturally on some occasions, be genealogically particularly useful.

It should be mentioned that these series continue after the end of the 'Company era' for the mustering of soldiers, N.C.O.s and Warrant Officers of the Commissariat or 'Unattached Lists' (described later). Although such lists contain an increasingly large number of soldiers who had never served in the Company's Armies, it does feature details of those who had transferred from those armies in 1861

12. Soldiers' Wives and Children

The Company admitted about six percent married soldier recruits and took their wives, plus any children, to India with their husbands in their troopships. These wives and children were considered to be 'on the strength' of the corps to which the husband was appointed. In India, a number of additional soldiers married, provided that they obtained the written permission of their Commanding Officer. The total number of wives 'on the strength' seems typically to have been about ten percent and they, plus all children under 14 years, were included on the 'Monthly Musters' of the husband's company. These muster records do not survive.

An allowance was paid to each husband for his wife and for each child under the age of 14 years: see next page for an extract from the General Orders by Government summarising this. Once a child achieved his or her 14th birthday, it was considered that they were capable of finding their own way in life. For boys, particularly in the earlier years, this commonly meant that they joined the army themselves, possibly as a drummer or bugler. Girls were, naturally, unable to do this. A few were accepted into service but the majority needed to find a husband, preferably one who could arrange with his Commanding Officer to have them 'mustered' with his regiment, and thereby gain the benefits of this. It is for this reason that a high proportion of marriages is noted in which the bride is only 14 years of age.

To find a husband was generally no problem either for a 14 year-old girl or for a young widow. Thousands of young soldiers were brought to India each year as recruits and most would eventually seek a wife. A young Christian European or Anglo-Indian girl would have found herself confronted by a large number of suitors. Many soldiers were able to marry a native Indian woman but, generally, it was expected that she first became a Christian.

The climate, disease and warfare to which a soldier and his wife were subjected in India, especially when 'on the march', caused a high incidence of widowhood. The anxiety of a widowed soldier to find a new wife, particularly if left with young children, and the anxiety of a widow to find a new husband to protect her, caused rapid remarriages. These were generally agreed by the Commanding Officer and confirmed as soon as a chaplain could be found upon arrival at the destination. So, the first place to look for a re-marriage of a widow is in the same regiment as her former husband – and relatively rapidly after his passing.

A soldier's widow, who was mustered with her former husband's regiment, was entitled to a pension from the 'Lord Clive Fund', both for herself and for her children, unless and until she remarried (see Section 16 below). Unlike other pension funds, the Lord Clive Fund did not grant pensions individually to children but, no doubt, the widow's grant was intended to cover her children also. Pensions for some women have survived in 'Military Proceedings'. All applications had to be made and approved formally but such entries are haphazard at best.

As an interesting adjunct, several reasonably educated soldiers' wives were employed as school-teachers. Others became servants or nannies to officers' wives or other ladies. Several instances have been found where a soldier's wife would leave him in India to accompany her lady home to England and then, by recommendation, accompany another lady back to India and there be reunited with her husband. Applications for such employment often appeared in the major newspapers.

Allowances for Soldiers' Wives, Widows and Children

Extract from General Orders by the Right Honourable the Governor in Council

G.O. No.6 of 1841   Fort St. George, Madras 12 January 1841

20. An allowance of Rs. 5 per mensem is authorized to be drawn for the wives of effective, non-effective and pensioned European non-commissioned and inferior grades of the Honourable Company's service, such women being born of European parents.

21. An allowance of Rs. 3 ½ per mensem is authorized to East Indian wives of effective, non-effective and pensioned European non-commissioned and inferior grades of the Honourable Company's service, such women being the daughters of European soldiers who have been educated at Regimental or other established Military schools, and also to East Indian women, wives of Drummers, Buglers, etc., the offspring of European fathers married to women of the same description.

N.B. This boon is extended to all East Indian women who were wives of European Soldiers, etc. as above on 1st November 1840 without reference to parentage or place of education. It will be extended as an indulgence to claimants married subsequently to that date who can produce a certificate from a clergyman or other Public Functionary stating that such instruction as the daughter of a Christian soldier should receive has been bestowed on her, but each case must be submitted for the consideration and order of Government.

22. An allowance of Rupees 2 ½ per mensem for each child of an effective, non-effective and pensioned European non-commissioned officer or soldier of the Honourable Company's Service is authorized to be drawn for those under *fourteen* years of age, on attainment of which, or earlier should they be provided for, the allowance will cease.

23. Widows of deceased soldiers as described in paragraphs 20 and 21 will be entitled to draw an allowance of Rupees 5 and 3 ½ respectively for 6 months after the decease of their husbands, provided they remain so long in India, or until their admission on Lord Clive's Fund provided it takes place within 6 months; beyond which period this allowance will in no instance be payable without the sanction of Government.

Schooling for Children of Soldiers

Extract from General Orders by Government 13 April 1841

Children of Company soldiers upwards of 4 years of age are required to attend the Regimental School when there happens to be one at the Station to which the Parents are attached. The Children of Company Soldiers of the Roman Catholic persuasion are not, however, to be compelled to attend in opposition to the wishes of the Parents.

12.1 Military Orphanages (Asylums)

As one might expect, sadly often children were left alone by the death of or simple abandonment by their parents. In each of the three presidencies, Orphanages – called 'Asylums' – were established for both boys and girls so abandoned. Entrance was limited to children of European or Anglo-Indian Christians. In Calcutta there was an 'Upper Orphan School' for children of European Officers and Department Officers and a 'Lower Orphan School' for children of European Warrant Officers, N.C.O.s and Other Ranks. Registers or Lists of inmates do not routinely survive. However, the 'Bengal Military Orphans' Society' kept a list of the boys of the Calcutta Asylum for Pension purposes. The lists may be seen in IOR reference L/AG/23/7/2-9 and 14 (LDS Film No.1866779 – 82)

One further exception has been uncovered. This is for the girls of the 'Madras Military Female Asylum' prior to 1839, for which there is a limited list, and for those in attendance in 1839, which is believed to be a full list. This list may be found in IOR Reference F/4/1855.

In a number of instances, the names of children granted admission to the Asylum were printed in the major presidency newspapers of the day.

The asylums provided a good practical education for the children so that they would be able to stand on their own feet when released at the age of 14. From 1792, the Madras Military Male Asylum was assisted by the government to establish a printing press and was sponsored by them to print almost all of their official printed papers. Even today, researchers will be familiar with documents printed for the Madras Presidency by the 'Asylum Press'.

In 1871, responsibility for the asylums was taken over by the Lawrence foundation.

12.2 Military Schools

By Government decree dated 6th April 1830, each corps of the Army was instructed to provide schooling for its children, premises were provided and funds were allocated for a teacher, books, etc. Most regiments appointed a 'Schoolmaster Serjeant' who undertook responsibility for the education of both the children of the regiment and of the soldiers themselves. Frequently, teaching of children was entrusted to one or more of the soldiers' wives of that corps. Very infrequently, references to individual teachers may be found in sources such as General Orders but the regular references in the Monthly Muster Lists of the individual corps have not survived.

It was not compulsory that children attend these schools and the choice whether or not to do so was left to the father of the child concerned. Evidently, he would have been most unwise not to insist that his child attend. Experience indicates that such schooling was generally of a high standard. The quality of hand-writing of former pupils is generally found to have been exemplary and instances may be found of former pupils obtaining senior teaching posts themselves.

By further order of Government, dated 13th April 1841, all children above the age of 4 years were required to attend their regimental school. However, no doubt due to the significant amount of religious content of the teaching, Roman Catholic children were not compelled to attend if their parents did not wish it (see page 48, last para).

13. Soldiers' Discharge

13.1 Pre-Mutiny Discharge

Prior to the 'India Act' of 1858, soldiers were granted discharges for several reasons:

a. They were wounded too severely to enable them to continue in service
b. They were ill or exhausted by service and could be classed as 'worn out'
c. They bought themselves out of their service
d. The period of service for which they had signed up had expired

In such instances they were entitled to be repatriated 'home' and the Company paid the costs of their voyage back to the place of their enlistment.

Details of soldiers discharged and returned to England from 1830 to 1861 and beyond (to 1882), for all three presidencies, are all to be found in the Bengal Presidency records. These are:

Years	IOR Reference	LDS Film No.
1830 – 1856	L/MIL/10/301	1867204
1856 – 1882	L/MIL/10/302	1867204
1861 – 1882	L/MIL/10/302	1867205

Examples of the content of these records are given below. Remember, these records are distinct from those which apply to an option to accept discharge with bounty following the India Act of 1858.

Examples of details provided in L/MIL/10/301

Discharge Papers of Soldiers who returned to England (1849)

Name:	Peter Evers	Joseph Bather
Rank:	Bombardier	Gunner
Service:	21 y. 0 mo.	3 y. 10 mo.
Presidency:	Madras	Bengal
Age:	44	24
Height:	5 ft. 7 1/2 ins	5 ft. 7 ins
Complexion:	Fair	Fresh
Visage:	Round	Oval
Eyes:	Hazel	Light Blue
Hair:	Brown	Brown
Trade:	Weaver	Wheelwright
Character:	Good	----
County:	Drogheda	Chester
Per Ship:	'Vernon', 21 June 1849	'Prince of Wales', 22 June 1849
Where Enlisted:	Drogheda	Liverpool
Marching Money:	£ 1. 0s. 0d.	----
Cause of Discharge:	Time Expired	Discharge Purchased

13.2 Soldiers Opting for Post-Mutiny Discharge (1858-1860)

Following discussions with his officer in order to ensure that he understood the implications of both options, a soldier had to make the choice within a minimum period of 30 days. Those then opting for discharge were asked to sign an undertaking, an example of which, taken at random, is given at the end of the following list. Arrangements were then made for settlement of monies owed to him, including payment of his bounty, and for his embarkation for England. The Discharge Papers are extensive and include – in one place - copies of the details of his recruitment, service and discharge. They may be found in pieces listed below:

Papers of Soldiers Discharged with Bounty 1859-1861

Bengal

Unit	Ref. Nos.	IOR Ref.	LDS Film No.
1st Bengal Light Cavalry	1-722	L/MIL/10/303	1867085
1st Bengal Light Cavalry	723-End	L/MIL/10/303	1867086
2nd Bengal Light Cavalry	1-565	L/MIL/10/304	1867086
2nd Bengal Light Cavalry	566-1417	L/MIL/10/304	1867087
2nd Bengal Light Cavalry	1418-End	L/MIL/10/304	1867088
3rd Bengal Light Cavalry	1-299	L/MIL/10/305	1867088
3rd Bengal Light Cavalry	300-End	L/MIL/10/305	1867089
4th Bengal Light Cavalry	1-304	L/MIL/10/306	1867089
4th Bengal Light Cavalry	305-1207	L/MIL/10/306	1867090
4th Bengal Light Cavalry	1208-End	L/MIL/10/306	1867091
5th Bengal Light Cavalry	1-679	L/MIL/10/307	1867091
5th Bengal Light Cavalry	680-End	L/MIL/10/307	1867092
Bengal Artillery	1-600	L/MIL/10/308	1867092
Bengal Artillery	600-1351	L/MIL/10/308	1867135
Bengal Artillery	1352-2098	L/MIL/10/308	1867136
Bengal Artillery	2099-2851	L/MIL/10/308	1867137
Bengal Artillery	2852-3602	L/MIL/10/308	1867138
Bengal Artillery	3603-4350	L/MIL/10/308	1867139
Bengal Artillery	4351-5101	L/MIL/10/308	1867140
Bengal Artillery	5102-5848	L/MIL/10/308	1867141
Bengal Artillery	5849-End	L/MIL/10/308	1867181
1st Bengal Fusiliers	1-147	L/MIL/10/309	1867181
1st Bengal Fusiliers	148-729	L/MIL/10/309	1867182
1st Bengal Fusiliers	730-End	L/MIL/10/309	1867183
2nd Bengal Fusiliers	1-554	L/MIL/10/310	1867183
2nd Bengal Fusiliers	555-End	L/MIL/10/310	1867184
3rd Bengal Infantry	1-749	L/MIL/10/311	1867184
3rd Bengal Infantry	750-End	L/MIL/10/311	1867185
4th Bengal Infantry	All	L/MIL/10/312	1867186
5th Bengal Infantry	1-162	L/MIL/10/313	1867186
5th Bengal Infantry	163-End	L/MIL/10/313	1867187
6th Bengal Infantry	All	L/MIL/10/314	1867187

Unit	Ref. Nos.	IOR Ref.	LDS Film No.
Bengal Sappers and Miners, and Engineers	All	L/MIL/10/315	1867187
Bengal Local Infantry	All	L/MIL/10/316	1867187
Bengal Invalids	All	L/MIL/10/317	1867204

Madras

Unit	Surname Initials.	IOR Ref.	LDS Film No.
Madras Artillery	A - Mc	L/MIL/11/278	1886124
Madras Artillery	Mc - Z	L/MIL/11/278	1886125
1st Madras Fusiliers	All	L/MIL/11/279	1886125
2nd Madras Infantry	H - Z	L/MIL/11/280	1886141*
3rd Madras Infantry	F - K	L/MIL/11/281	1886141*
3rd Madras Infantry	K - Z	L/MIL/11/281	1886142

* Note the limited range. The remainder are unfortunately missing..

Bombay

Unit	Ref Nos.	IOR Ref.	LDS Film No.
Bombay Artillery	1 - 310	L/MIL/12/282	2029780
Bombay Artillery	311 - 930	L/MIL/12/282	2029751
Bombay Artillery	931 - 1691	L/MIL/12/282	2029781
Jager Corps	1-84	L/MIL/12/283	2029782
1st Bombay Fusiliers	1 - 600	L/MIL/12/284	2029782
1st Bombay Fusiliers	601 - 638	L/MIL/12/284	2029783
2nd Bombay Infantry	1 - 581	L/MIL/12/285	2029783
3rd Bombay Infantry	1 - 637	L/MIL/12/286	2029840

Section 13 Soldiers' Discharge

Papers of a Soldier Voluntarily Discharged with Bounty 1859-1861

Extract from IOR Ref: L/MIL/11/278 Folio 252 et seq. (LDS Film No.: 1886124)

Service Report of Regimental Committee

The Honourable Company's Madras Regiment of Horse Artillery, Saugor 15th August 1859.

Proceedings of a Regimental Committee held this day for the purpose of verifying by recording the services of conduct, character and cause of discharge of No. 4321, William Cunningham, Gunner in the Horse Brigade of the regiment above mentioned.

President: Captain Henry Erskine Hicks, Madras Artillery.
Captain R.G.F. Henigan, Madras Horse Artillery. Lieut. C. Johnson, Madras Horse Artillery

The Committee having examined and compared the Regimental records, the Soldier's Book, and such other documents as appeared to them to be necessary, report that *William Cunningham*, G. No. *4321*, by trade a *Labourer*, was born in the parish of *King's* in or near the town of *Cloghane* in the County of *King's* and was attested for the EIC Regiment of Artillery at *Dublin on 10th October 1853* at the age of *twenty* years, that of making every deduction required by the regulations, the service up to this day which he is entitled to reckon amounts to *5 years 311* days as shown by the detailed statement on the second page......and further that discharge is proposed under provisions of GGO No. 883, dated 20th June 1859.

With regard to the character and conduct of William Cunningham, the Committee have to report that upon reference to the Defaulters' Book and by the testimony that has been given, it appears that his character is good. Served with the Saugor Field Division in Bundelkund, present at the attack on Ghilling 10th, Skirmish Kubai on the 17th, Battle of Bandah 19th and attack on Jaimpoor on 26th April 1858. Relief of Renimn 25th and Storming the Heights of Purananon on 27th December 1858.

--ooOOoo--

Declaration

I, *William Cunningham*, in the Regiment of Artillery, hereby declare that I do of my own free will request to be discharged from the Honourable Company's Service and I further declare that a period of not less than thirty days has elapsed since I made application for my discharge, and it has been fully explained to me, and I perfectly understand, that on receiving my discharge at my own request I entirely relinquish all claim to pension and that if I should re-enlist, my past services prior to the date of my present discharge can not be allowed to reckon for the purpose of obtaining any pensionary benefit.

Signed   Signed

Soldier   President

Signed in the presence of the Regimental Committee at Saugor this twenty-seventh day of August 1859.

Certificate:

This certifies that the bearer hereof *Gunner William Cunningham of the Horse Brigade, Madras Artillery* of *25 11/12* years of age, 5 ft. 8 ½ ins. high, *Fair* hair, *Fresh* complexion ----- visage, *blue* eyes, by trade a *labourer*, a Native of *Cloghane* in the County of *King's* and Kingdom of *Ireland*, enlisted at *Dublin* on *10th October 1853* hath served in Her Majesty's Indian Army justly and truly for the space of *5* years and *11* months *and 4 days* and is hereby discharged at his Request being unwilling to serve in H.M.'s Indian Forces.

Having first received a full and true account of all his Pay, Arrears of Pay, Clothing and all other Demands whatever from the time of his first enlisting to the present date, as appears by his receipt on the other side hereof.

Given under my hand at Fort Saint George, Madras this *20th* day of *September 1859*

By Order: H Marshall, Col.
Ag. Secretary to Government,
Military Department.

--ooOOoo--

13.3 Soldiers Opting for Transfer to the British Army (1858-1860)

Soldiers who opted to join the Queen's Army at this stage would have their continuing records amongst those of the British Army records in the War Office records (WO series) at The National Archives (Public Record Office) at Kew. To aid the location of these men within the records there, the re-naming of the various Corps, given in table 5, should prove useful. In fact, many of the regiments and battalions remained in India for a number of years before they were sent elsewhere.

Lists of the volunteers for this service are to be found in:

Presidency	Service	IOR Reference	LDS Film No.
Bengal	Cavalry	L/MIL/10/324	Not filmed
	Artillery	L/MIL/10/325	Not filmed
	Infantry	L/MIL/10/326	Not filmed
Madras	A. Warrant Officers		
	B. All Corps	L/MIL/11/282	1886142
Bombay	All	L/MIL/12/288	Not filmed

14. An Introduction to Military Pension Schemes

14.1 The 'Lord Clive Pensions'

In 1766 and 1767 Robert, Lord Clive allocated part of the money that he had received as a result of his activities in Bengal, to the funding of pensions under certain conditions, to European Officers and 'other ranks', and their widows, that had served, and were yet to serve, in the Company's armies. Although soldiers were supposed to be 'unfit for further service' to qualify, in practice the pension was granted to time-expired soldiers, whatever their state of health. The pension was not particularly generous, being equivalent to the British soldier's Chelsea Pension. This fund became referred to as 'The Lord Clive Fund' and the promise of a pension at the end of their service was a significant factor in the recruitment of soldiers to the Company's armies. It may be mentioned that admission to the fund was subject to a 'means test'. Since they were generally of sufficient independent means, officers would not be awarded a pension from the Lord Clive fund and therefore many do not appear in the fund records. Essentially, of course, all soldiers qualified for a pension from the fund.

Whilst the details of the fund were being established until implemented in 1770, the bequests were gaining significant monetary interest. This accumulated interest was applied to the creation of a 'Contingent Fund' permitting pensions to be paid to certain soldiers and their widows ineligible, for various reasons, to receive one from the main fund.

The regulations of the fund, which was non-contributory, provided a pension to Officers and Warrant Officers of half of their service pay. Other ranks were entitled to the same amount as that awarded to Chelsea Pensioners, i.e. those soldiers retired from the British Army.

Many men did not, of course, survive to receive a pension but, in this case, an allowance from the fund was paid to their widows for themselves and their children. This continued for as long as the wife lived, or unless and until she re-married, and until the children reached their fourteenth birthday. Many soldiers who retired from the Company's armies prior to its disbandment in 1861 (see section 5) continued in retirement well after that date and the Government continued to honour the payment of their pensions. Although those ultimately responsible for paying pensions changed, the records of payment are effectively continuous.

As regards officers, the Lord Clive Fund is only the first of several military pensions series. There are also the regular service pensions, first granted in 1796, the 'off-reckonings', and the five official Military Funds for widows and children. The Lord Clive Fund records extend as far as 1937, when the last pensioner died.

14.2 Pensions in General

Although valuable sources of information for the genealogist, the pension records are not always easy to follow. Records of the award and payment of a pension depend upon the recipient's date of retirement, chosen place of retirement (Europe, India or the Colonies) and to some extent his rank. Further complication is introduced if he elected to change his place of retirement. For example, several pensioners elected to return 'home' to the UK upon retirement, only to return to India at a later date. In such cases it may not be simple to trace his pension payments.

This leads to six general rules:

a. Payment records are not generally available for pensions paid in India, except to widows. To offset this disadvantage, records of the continued presence in India of Officers and Warrant Officers are available in the Presidency Almanacs and Directories. Pensioned soldiers may be found in the 'Pensioners' section of the Annual Muster Lists. This will include Warrant Officers after 1861 when they had transferred to the Indian Army

b. Some senior officers, Lieutenant-Colonels and above, were not technically considered to have retired and continued to receive the full pay to which they were entitled as serving officers. Such monies were called 'off-reckonings', from 1803, or 'Colonel's Allowances' from 1852. As an alternative, a senior officer could also receive a regular pension but never in addition to a colonel's allowance. Payment records of these are available in IOR Series L/AG/21/12/1 to 46 (believed unfilmed by the LDS) for 1806 to 1948.

c. There is usually a clear distinction between Service Pensions (available in respect of an officer's service) and Provident, or Family Pensions, awarded for the maintenance of his widow and children. Occasionally, a fund, such as the Lord Clive Fund combined elements of both.

d. A number of independent or unofficial Pension Schemes were established for officers, particularly following the end of the Company era. It is doubtful if the records of these still exist, but, even if they do, they are not available either in the IOR or in the LDS Films. If an ancestor was known to be alive at a certain date and living in Europe but no pension payment is found, it is possible that he had subscribed to one of these.

e. It must be said that the logic behind the pension records is not always clear to 21st Century eyes. It will be seen that the records are split between several different series in the IOR but it should be said in their defence that they are much simpler, better organized and explained than they were a few years ago. Therefore, although it is recommended that you research the series indicated in sections 15 or 16 below, it may always be advisable to consult other sources in related series if you are unsuccessful!

f. Finally, the majority of records are distributed between two series: L/AG/21 (mostly allocated to Payments) and L/AG/23 (mostly allocated to Administration, often with data concerning the recipient). Although many of the latter series have been filmed by the LDS, those of the former series have not. Researchers wishing to consult the former are therefore obliged to do so at the IOR itself. It is not at all the purpose of this book to transcribe the complete IOR Catalogue. Nevertheless, as an aid to preparing a visit to the IOR, the general breakdown of what may be found in the L/AG/21 series relating to pensions is provided on the next page.

Summary of L/AG/ series Pension Payment Records
(Not filmed by the LDS)

These important records are available only at the India Office Records Section at the British Library, since they were not filmed by the LDS. They are presented here to advise researchers of their existence and to recommend their consultation, if possible.

L/AG/9/4	Authorities for Warrants (Pensions and Annuities &c to Officers)	(1788 – 1860)
L/AG/10/33/55 to 57	Pensions to 'Other Ranks'	(1846 – 1875)
L/AG/20/6	Officers' Furlough Books	(1795 – 1947)
L/AG/21/10/4 to 16	Quarterly Pension Payment Books (Officers and Widows)	(1860 – 1886)
L/AG/21/10/35 to 41	Pensions to Widows of 'Other Ranks'.	(1820 – 1869)
L/AG/21/11/1 to 18	Pensions and Payment Books (Europe Only)	(1825 – 1860)
L/AG/21/12/1 to 46	Senior Officers' 'Off-Reckonings'.	(1803 – 1948)
L/AG/21/15	Medical Service Pensions and Annuities	(1825 – 1948)
L/AG/21/26	Bengal Military Fund Payments	(1842 – 1968)
L/AG/21/27/4-5	Bengal Orphan Fund See also L/AG/23/7/10-12	(1881 – 1886)
L/AG/21/29	Madras Medical Fund Pensions	(1849 – 1955)
L/AG/21/30	Madras Military Fund Payments	(1842 – 1909)
L/AG/21/32	Bombay Military Fund Payments	(1851 – 1968)
L/AG/21/44	Pensions payable in British Colonies	(1860 – 1928)
L/AG/21/45/1 to 8	Pensions Payments to Other Ranks and Widows	(1882 – 1937)
L/AG/26/14	Admissions to Pension of Dept. and Warrant Officers	(1883 – 1914)
L/AG/26/15	Admissions/Cancellations/Restorations to Pensions of Widows of Department and Warrant Officers	(1883 – 1908)
L/AG/35/50 to 54	Payment Registers, Other Ranks and Widows	(1829 – 1881)

15. Officers' Pension Records

15.1 Officers' Admissions to Pension (Not including Warrant Officers)

For officers who retired to the United Kingdom between 1799 and 1835, 'Auditor's Reference' IOR series D/153 to 252 (thought unfilmed by LDS) contain formal requests by officers to retire on pension. Several of these contain summaries of their services written by officers themselves. These records are indexed in Z/D/28 to 32.

Certificates were issued to an officer when he retired (from 1836 to 1857, extended to 1896 for the Bengal Army only). An index to these is provided in Z/L/MIL/10/3-4 (LDS Film No. 1886143), and the certificates themselves in L/MIL/10/108 to 112 (LDS Film No. 1867391). Note that, although the L/MIL/10 series is generally limited to the Bengal Army, these particular records cover officers from all three presidencies.

The major series of pension records are those for the Lord Clive Fund, which range from 1770 to 1867. They cover both Officers and Soldiers – plus their widows where appropriate. Only officers' widows are given until 1826 (Bengal), 1800 (Madras) and 1830 (Bombay). These records are given in detail in Section 16.3

15. 2 Payment of Pension in India

It should be mentioned once more that there are no particular documents recording the payment of pensions to officers and soldiers who remained in India. Their presence is generally recorded in Army Lists and in Presidency Almanacs and Directories.

15.3 Payment of Pension to Officers (including Department and Warrant Officers) and their Widows in Europe (UK)

Some service pensions were first awarded to the Company's military officers prior to a re-establishment of the rules in 1796. These are recorded in "Authorities for Payment of Warrants" among other payments such as annuities, in the Accountant General's records L/AG/9/4/1-12. They stretch from 1788 to 1860 but because regrettably there are no indexes, it is necessary to know the approximate date of the man's retirement and to search in roughly chronological order. This means that they are mainly useful for the earlier years, before other records become available.

The rules introduced in 1796 allowed an officer to retire on full pay if he had served in India for 25 years, which included three years furlough. If he had served less than 25 years, but more than 9, he would have been permitted to retire on grounds of poor health at a reduced pension – generally half the pay of the final rank that he had achieved.

Although these pensions had been introduced in 1796, the routine payment books only survive in the India Office Records from 1825 onwards. However, formal requests for admission to pension over the years 1799 to 1835 are to be found in the Auditor's References D/153 to 252. Fortunately, these are indexed in Z/D/28 to 32.

It has to be stated that the LDS appear not to have filmed any of the L/AG/9/ series nor of the 'D' series. These must, therefore be consulted at the India Office Records. As earlier indicated, the same applies to the extensive L/AG/21 series, featuring the following records:-

Payments to officers and their widows from the Lord Clive Fund may be found in L/AG/9/28-30 for 1849 to 1860, followed by L/AG/21/10/4-41 from Oct 1860 to Mar 1886.

The Main Series of Payment Books for those Officers (including Department and Warrant Officers) who retired to Europe at the end of their service are to be found in the L/AG/21/11 series which, in view of their importance, are given in greater detail below. Note that the two lists are mostly contained in the same documents but there are some inconsistencies.

Pension Payments to Officers in Europe (including Departmental and Warrant Officers)

Payment Book Reference	Presidency	Dates for Officers	Dates for Department & Warrant Officers
L/AG/21/11/1	All	1825 – 1827	1825 – 1827
L/AG/21/11/2	All	1828 – 1830	1828 – 1830
L/AG/21/11/3	All	1831 – 1834	1831 – 1834
L/AG/21/11/4	All	1834 – 1838	1834 – 1838
L/AG/21/11/5	Bengal	1838 – 1846	1838 – 1846
L/AG/21/11/5	Madras	1838 – 1846	1838 – 1842
L/AG/21/11/6	Bengal	1846 – 1848	1846 – 1848
L/AG/21/11/7	Bengal	1848 – 1854	1848 – 1854
L/AG/21/11/8	Bengal	1854 – 1858	
L/AG/21/11/9	Bengal	1858 – 1860	
L/AG/21/11/11	Madras	1842 – 1848	1842 – 1848
L/AG/21/11/12	Madras	1848 – 1854	1848 – 1854
L/AG/21/11/13	Madras	1854 – 1860	
L/AG/21/11/14	Madras	1860	
L/AG/21/11/15	Bombay	1838 – 1848	1838 – 1848
L/AG/21/11/16	Bombay	1848 – 1854	1848 – 1854
L/AG/21/11/17	Bombay	1854 – 1859	1854 – 1859
L/AG/21/11/17	Bengal		1854 – 1859
L/AG/21/11/17	Madras		1854 – 1859
L/AG/21/11/18	Bombay	1859 – 1860	
L/AG/21/11/18	Bengal		1859 – 1860
L/AG/21/11/18	Madras		1859 – 1860

These two series continue after 1860. That for Officers are retained in L/AG/21/11. That for Department and Warrant Officers in a mixture of L/AG/21/11 and L/AG/21/15. From 1893, the latter change to series L/AG/21/13.

Officers who had joined the service before 1831 and who had commanded a regiment as Lieutenant Colonel (although they may have subsequently risen higher) never technically retired. They were entitled to receive a 'Colonel's Allowance' instead of a pension. Records of the Colonels' Allowances may be found in the Accountant General's series L/AG/21/12 (No LDS Films). Other high ranking officers, for instance those who spent their career in Staff positions, would have received a regular military pension.

15.4 Family Pension Funds

Each of the three Presidencies established a pension fund for the widows and families of officers in its army. These were set up in 1824 (Bengal), 1808 (Madras) and 1816 (Bombay) and all officers, whether married or bachelors, were obliged to contribute shortly after their establishment. These schemes were closed to new subscribers in 1862. Indexes and/or Rolls of subscribers are separately listed below, together with the references and Film Nos. recording personal details of applicants and their payments. Note that, as for other pension payments, no records are available if the widow and her children remained in India.

These records contain information, such as the location of recipients, names and ages of children, etc. which may not easily be found elsewhere. Indeed, in the case of the Madras Military Fund, an excellent card index summary of officers and their families has been produced (1981) by Anthony Farrington and Margaret Makepeace, of L/AG/23/10/1-2. This is to be found on the open shelves at the IOR Reading Room (355.332), and the officers' roll may be consulted on the A2A website, as described on page 15. Included in the Madras records are a large number (1400) of applicants who were required to furnish certificates of baptism, marriage and death (L/AG/23/10/11 to 13c, LDS Films 1866806 and 807). These records have been transcribed by Peter Hart and Sylvia Murphy of Sydney Australia and are now available in the FIBIS searchable database at: www.search.fibis.org.

Military Fund (Officers) Family Pensions

Bengal Military Fund (Established 1824. Closed to new subscribers 1862)

IOR Reference	Description	LDS Film No.
Pensioner Lists		
L/AG/23/6/1	Roll of subscribers 1824	1886713
L/AG/23/6/2	List of Widows 1806	1886713
L/AG/23/6/3	Registers of Pensioners & Payments 1866-1871	1836134
L/AG/23/6/4	Registers of Pensioners & Payments 1872-1876	1836134
L/AG/23/6/5	Registers of Pensioners & Payments 1877-1881	1836136
L/AG/23/6/6	Registers of widows post-1887	1836136
L/AG/23/6/7	Ledger of subscriptions paid in UK 1860-1866	1836136 & 37
L/AG/23/6/8-11	Ledger of subscriptions paid in UK 1867-1909	1866775 & 76
L/AG/23/6/12	Index to Fund in L/AG/23/6/8-11	1836137
L/AG/23/6/13	Ledgers of Subscribers as at 1 Jan. 1860	1866776
L/AG/23/6/14-20	Authorities for Payments in the UK 1860-1892	1866777 & 78
Payment Lists (Note some repetitions of above for records where data are combined)		
L/AG/21/26/1	Pension Payment Book 1842-1852	Not Filmed
L/AG/21/26/2	Pension Payment Book 1852-1857	Not Filmed
L/AG/21/26/3	Pension Payment Book 1857-1860	Not Filmed
L/AG/23/6/14	Pension Payment Book 1860-1863	1866776 & 77
L/AG/23/6/15	Pension Payment Book 1863-1866	1866777
L/AG/23/6/3	Pension Payment Book 1866-1871	1836134
L/AG/23/6/4	Pension Payment Book 1872-1876	1836134
L/AG/23/6/5	Pension Payment Book 1877-1881	1836134
L/AG/21/26/9-18	UK Payments 1881 – 1900	Not Filmed

Madras Military Fund (Established 1808. Closed to new subscribers 1862)

IOR Reference	Description	LDS Film No.

Pensioner Lists

L/AG/23/10/1	Rolls of Subscribers and their families	1850712
L/AG/23/10/2	Rolls of Subscribers and their families	1850713
L/AG/23/10/7	Registers of Pensioners & Payments 1866-1871	1850714
L/AG/23/10/8	Registers of Pensioners & Payments 1872-1876	1850714
L/AG/23/10/9 Pt.1	Registers of Pensioners & Payments 1877-1881	1850714
L/AG/23/10/9 Pt.2	Registers of Pensioners admitted before Jun 1882	1850715
L/AG/23/10/10/Pt.1	Registers of Pensioners admitted after Jan. 1882	1850715
L/AG/23/10/10/Pt.2	Registers of Pensioners admitted up to the 1960's	1850715
L/AG/23/10/11	Personal details (BMD Certificates Nos. 1-400)	1866806
L/AG/23/10/12	Personal details (BMD Certificates Nos. 401-850)	1866807
L/AG/23/10/13a	Personal details (BMD Certificates Nos. 851-980)	1866807
L/AG/23/10/13a	Personal details (BMD Certificates Nos. 981-1200)	1866877
L/AG/23/10/13b	Personal details (BMD Certificates Nos. 1201-1300)	1866877
L/AG/23/10/13c	Personal details (BMD Certificates Nos. 1301-1400)	1866877

Payment Lists (Note some repetitions of above for records where data are combined)

L/AG/21/30/1	UK Payments Books 1842 – 1849	Not Filmed
L/AG/21/30/2	UK Payments Books 1849 – 1852	Not Filmed
L/AG/21/26/2	UK Payments Books 1852 – 1857	Not Filmed
L/AG/21/26/3	UK Payments Books 1857 – 1860	Not Filmed
L/AG/23/10/14	Authority for Payments in the UK (1860-1863)	1866877
L/AG/23/10/15	Authority for Payments in the UK (1863-1866)	1866877 - 78
L/AG/23/10/16	Authority for Payments in the UK (1866-1867)	1866878
L/AG/23/10/17	Authority for Payments in the UK (1868-1873)	1866878
L/AG/23/10/18	Abstracts of Miscellaneous Payments (1866-1879)	1866879
L/AG/23/10/19	Abstracts of Miscellaneous Payments (1879-1913)	1866879
L/AG/23/11/1	Registers of Madras Pensioners (1877 - 1888)	1850714
L/AG/21/30/10-20	UK Payments Books 1881 – 1903	Not Filmed

Madras Medical Fund - Administration

L/AG/23/9/1	Family Register of Pensioners and Payments (1870-1879)	1850712
L/AG/23/9/2	Family Register of Pensioners and Payments (1880-1881)	1850712
L/AG/23/9/3	Family Register of Pensioners and Payments (c. 1872))	1850712

Madras Medical Fund – Payments

L/AG/21/29/1-41 Pensions Payment Registers (1849 – 1955)   Not Filmed

Bombay Military Fund (Established 1816. Closed to new subscribers 1862)

IOR Reference	Description	LDS Film No.
Pensioner Lists		
L/AG/23/12/1-4	List of Subscribers from 1824-1892	1850760-62
L/AG/23/12/5	Index to L/AG/23/12/1-4	1850762
L/AG/23/12/6	Alphabetical Subscribers Lists, 1858, 1866 & 1875	1850762
L/AG/23/12/10	Register of Pensioners & Payments 1866-1871	1850763
L/AG/23/12/11	Register of Pensions & Payments, 1872-1876	1850763
L/AG/23/12/12	Register of Pensions & Payments, 1877-1881, plus Register of Pensioners admitted before Feb. 1893	1850763 & 64
L/AG/23/12/13	Register of Pensioners admitted after Nov. 1892	1850764

Payment Lists (Note some repetitions of above for records where data are combined)

IOR Reference	Description	LDS Film No.
L/AG/21/32/1	Register of UK Payments 1851 – 1852	Not Filmed
L/AG/21/26/2	Register of UK Payments 1852 – 1857	Not Filmed
L/AG/21/26/3	Register of UK Payments 1857 – 1860	Not Filmed
No Record	Register of UK Payments 1860 – 1866	
L/AG/23/12/10	Register of Pensioners & Payments 1866-1871	1850763
L/AG/23/12/11	Register of Pensions and Payments, 1872-1876	1850763
L/AG/23/12/12	Register of Pensions and Payments, 1877-1881	1850763 & 64
L/AG/21/32/8-31	Register of UK Payments 1881 – 1946	Not Filmed

15.5 Bengal Military Orphan Society
In Bengal, there was established a fund for payments to the children of Bengal Army officers, surgeons and chaplains. This was not the case in Madras or Bombay.
The Bengal Military Orphan Fund was established in 1783 and made compulsory from 1807. It was closed to new subscribers in 1861. The records include lists of orphans, both legitimate and illegitimate, as follows:

IOR Reference	Description	LDS Film. No
L/AG/23/7/7	Alphabetical List of Orphans, c.1820 to 1857	1866780
L/AG/23/7/8	Alphabetical List of Orphans in England, 1818 to 1834	1866780
L/AG/23/7/9	Alphabetical List of Orphans in England, 1856 to 1866	1866780
L/AG/23/7/10-13	Registers of Orphans from 1866 to the end of the Fund.	1836135 & 36
L/AG/23/7/15-19	Registers of subscriptions with details of subscribers' children from 1856 to the end of the Fund (Indexed in L/AG/23/6/12)	1836137 & 1850622 1866776
L/AG/23/7/20	Returns of Births, Marriages and Deaths of Children Plus List of Orphans in India , 1877 to 1907	1850622
L/AG/21/27/4-5	Alphabetical List of Orphans, 1881 - 1886	Not Filmed
L/AG/21/26/1-64	Military Fund Payment Books, 1866 to 1968	Not Filmed

Officers, and their widows, who received pensions under the Lord Clive Fund may be found in series L/AG/21/10/35 to 41 (Half-yearly Registers of Payment, 1820 to 1860).

16. Soldiers' Pension Records

16.1 Admissions to Pension of Soldiers (including Warrant Officers)

Registers of Early Applications for Admission to Pension, mostly for NCO's and Privates (although with a few officers and widows) and for all three presidencies, are to be found in series L/AG/23/2/20 to 22 (LDS Film No. 1851027) from October 1772 to January 1798 (The breakdown is included in section 16.3 below, together with the 'Payment Records'). These apply to soldiers retiring to Europe. They are additionally useful, in cases in which the soldier may be missing from the Embarkation Lists, since they provide details of the soldier's previous service and of his place of origin.

Admissions to Pension of Soldiers are available for soldiers retiring from 1830 to 1882. These records provide the name, place of origin, former occupation and description of the soldier upon recruitment and are to be found in:

- L/AG/23/2/65 for 1830 to 1848 (LDS Film No. 1866549), which additionally provides recruitment details of each soldier, and
- L/AG/23/2/66 for 1849 to 1882 (LDS Film No. 1866549), which provides not only recruitment details but pensioners' towns of residence and includes widows from 1862.

Example – Soldiers' <u>Admissions</u> to Pensions

An example found in L/AG/23/2/66 is:

Regiment:	4th Battalion Artillery – Madras, Bombardier
No. in Pension List:	60
Name:	Peter Evers
Rate:	1/-
Date of Admission to Pension	27 June 1849
Height:	5 ft. 7 ½ ins.
Hair:	Brown
Eyes:	Hazel
Complexion:	Fair
Age:	46
Character, Trade or Occupation:	Good – Weaver
Period of Service:	21 years 0 months.
Cause of Discharge:	Time Expired
Place of Birth:	St. Peter's, Drogheda
Residence:	St. Peter's, Drogheda
Pension to commence:	21st to 30th June, 1849 inclusive
Remarks:	(None)

Note that there is no indication that this soldier's wife was still alive and entitled to a widow's pension if she later survived him.

16.2   Payment of Pensions in India

It should be mentioned once more that there are no particular payment books recording the payment of pensions to soldiers who remained in India. A pensioner's presence is generally recorded in the continuing Muster Lists. The researcher may pursue these year by year until the pensioner dies. When a soldier finally appears in the 'Casualties by Death' section of these lists, details are frequently provided of his estate and to whom this was entrusted, generally his wife. Other legatees are sometimes mentioned in these 'Casualties by Death' records, such as the soldier's mother or other relatives at home in England. These may provide genealogically important information.

16.3 Payment of Pension to Soldiers and their Widows in Europe

In parallel with the records of admission for soldiers was the establishment of 'Payment Registers'. These registers effectively track the fact that a retired soldier has been paid. These evidently cease at the time of his eventual death. A number of these registers, covering the years from 1829 to 1881 are retained in L/AG/35/50 to 54 (No LDS Film), but these appear chiefly to have been used to record a soldier's date of death. Payment Registers for soldiers, and their widows, who received pensions under the Lord Clive Fund may be found in series L/AG/21/10/35 to 41 for 1820 to 1860. The main records are to be found in series L/AG/23/2 from Items 41 to 61 and are followed by miscellaneous files as is set out, in this series, in full below, together with the application records referred to in Section 16.1.

Administration of Family Pension Funds - Lord Clive Pension Fund (1770 – 1867)

Presidency	IOR Reference	Dates of Entry*	LDS Film No.
General Applications of Other Ranks and their widows	L/AG/23/2/20	Oct 1772 – 1781 Mar	1851027
	L/AG/23/2/21	Oct 1791 – 1794 Sep	1851027
	L/AG/23/2/22	Sep 1794 – 1798 Jan	1851028
Half-yearly Payments to Pensioners All Ranks	L/AG/23/2/27**	Sep 1770 – 1808 Dec	1851028
	L/AG/23/2/28**	Nov 1816 – 1837 Apr	1851028
	L/AG/23/2/29**	May 1837 – 1857 Oct	1851028
	L/AG/23/2/30	Sep 1770 – 1785 Dec	1851028
	L/AG/23/2/31	Dec 1785 – 1797 Dec	1851029
	L/AG/23/2/32	Nov 1817 – 1822 Jan	1851029
	L/AG/23/2/33	Feb 1822 – 1826 Jan	1851029
	L/AG/23/2/34	Feb 1826 – 1830 Apr	1851029
	L/AG/23/2/35	May 1830 – 1833 Apr	1851029
	L/AG/23/2/36	May 1833 – 1836 Apr	1851029
	L/AG/23/2/37	Apr 1836 – 1839 Jan	1851029
	L/AG/23/2/38	Feb 1839 – 1843 Apr	1851030
	L/AG/23/2/39	Feb 1843 – 1846 Jan	1851030
	L/AG/23/2/40	Feb 1846 – 1848 Apr	1851030

* The dates quoted are dates of entry into the pension scheme. Naturally, payments continued until well after these dates

** Contingent Fund. The remainder are from the Capital Fund.

Lord Clive Pension Fund (1770 – 1867) (cont)

Bengal	L/AG/23/2/41	1779 – 1846	1851030-31
	L/AG/23/2/42	1847 – 1854	1851031
	L/AG/23/2/43	1854 – 1862	1851031
Madras	L/AG/23/2/44	1792 – 1818	1851031
	L/AG/23/2/44	1818 – 1824	1851032
	L/AG/23/2/45	1825 – 1832	1851032
	L/AG/23/2/46	1832 – 1834	1851032
	L/AG/23/2/47	1834 – 1838	1851033
	L/AG/23/2/48	1838 – 1840	1851033
	L/AG/23/2/49	1840 – 1844	1851034
	L/AG/23/2/50	1844 – 1847	1851034
	L/AG/23/2/51	1847 – 1849	1851034-5
	L/AG/23/2/52	1849 – 1851	1851035
	L/AG/23/2/53	1851 – 1862	1851035
	L/AG/23/2/54	1862 – 1864	1851036
	L/AG/23/2/55	1864	1851036
	L/AG/23/2/56	1865	1851036
	L/AG/23/2/57	1866	1851036
	L/AG/23/2/58	1866	1851036
	L/AG/23/2/59	1867	1851036
	L/AG/23/2/60	1867	1851036
Bombay	L/AG/23/2/61	1792 – 1863	1851036

General

Pensioners Receipts	L/AG/23/2/62	1822 – 1826	1851036
for London Pensions	L/AG/23/2/63	1826 – 1829	1851036
Marriage Certificate	L/AG/23/2/64	1819 – 1825	1866549
Justifications			
Admission Register	L/AG/23/2/65	1830 – 1849	1866549
to Pension in UK	L/AG/23/2/66	1849 – 1882	1866549
Registers of Dead or	L/AG/23/2/67	1828 – 1849	1866549
Removed Pensioners	L/AG/23/2/68	1849 – 1875	1866549
	L/AG/23/2/69	1877 – 1882	1866549

If a pensioned soldier elected to return to Europe, responsibility for payment of his pension passed to the Royal Hospital Chelsea, or the Royal Hospital Kilmainham for pensioners resident in Ireland. These payments were made alongside those to pensioners of the British Army and were available for collection at a variety of offices throughout the British Isles.

The records themselves may be viewed at The National Archives (TNA) at Kew in West London. They are to be found nominally in TNA War Office series WO22 and WO23 but also in WO97, WO116 to WO 121. Many of the WO97 series of records are available on TNA web-site at: www.nationalarchives.gov.uk.   As far as pensioners of the East India Company's armies are concerned, particularly in Ireland, the logic behind these is not always easy to identify. However, it is recommended that researchers persevere with their own logic until successful. As an example, having spent about a year of his retirement in India, Peter Evers, featured above, travelled 'home' to London and then on to his former residence in Drogheda in Ireland. He is first found in:

WO 23/21 Military Pensioners: East India Company's Service
(Payments made during years 1849 – 1858)

Name:	Peter Evers
No.	60
Corps:	Artillery
Rank:	Bombardier
Rate:	1s/-
Date of Admission:	1849 – 27th June
District:	1. East London
	2. Drogheda

Payments to Peter Evers continue in WO23/22 (1858-1865) with the same data, except that from 1860 onwards, he started to collect his pension in Newry instead of Drogheda. Next, they are recorded in WO23/23 (1866-1875). After this date, some change was made to the system of recording the payment and further records for Evers seem not to have survived. Regrettably, summary records at the IOR, L/AG/35/54 (No equivalent LDS Film) change at the same time and no further record of payment to Evers has been found. The Summary Records L/MIL/23/2/41 to 61, referred to above, changed at this date (1876) too and are missing from 1876 to 1882, when they re-commence. By this time Evers must have died.

Some soldiers elected to retire not in Britain but in one of Britain's various colonies around the world. Reference to their pension payments may sometimes be found in L/AG/23/2/67-69 for 1820 to 1862 (LDS Film No. 1866549). However, from 1860, payment of their pensions became the responsibility of the Government of the colony concerned and records may be found in L/AG/21/44 (No LDS Film).

As an addendum, it is of interest to note that retired Company soldiers were sometimes employed to act as guards in ships transporting convicts to New South Wales. Some further elected to remain there. Others opted for duty, in non-combatant roles, such as in the Crimea in 1854.

Additionally, Deaths of pensioners who retired to the United Kingdom from 1820 to 1882 may be found in L/AG/23/2/67-69, cited above. From 1850, these records give the district in the United Kingdom in which the death occurred. All of these records may be viewed on LDS Film No. 1866549. Alternatively, as already stated, dates of death for pensioners admitted from 1829 to 1881 may be found in L/AG/35/50 to 54

17. War Services

17.1 Company Records

This section applies to both Officers and Soldiers. Generally, the most complete information concerning an officer's conduct in a particular campaign or battle is to be gleaned from the military correspondence described in section 20.3. A list of the major wars and battles involving the Company's – and British – Armies in India is given in table 2. Most of such actions feature in the military correspondence which contains an assortment of reports from the Field Commander to his Presidency authorities and may be viewed at the IOR at the British Library. It must be said that it often requires significant study to obtain a good background and logical sequence of events.

If an action or campaign was worthy of the award of a medal, lists of those awarded such a medal are provided in various parts of IOR series L/MIL/5. Where relevant, these are included on page 68.

Furthermore, when a new territory was forcibly annexed to the control of the Company, its treasury was appropriated and 'surplus' funds distributed amongst all the officers and men who partook in the action to take it. A 'Prize Officer' was appointed to ensure that all troops got their allocated share. The amount of this 'Prize Money' received varied with rank according to a strictly established formula. Lists of those in receipt are generally available in the L/MIL/5 series. For interest, and by way of example, the following was distributed after the annexation of Coorg by the Madras Army in 1834 (L/MIL/5/258):

	Rupees-Annas-Pice
Colonels	27,928-10-11
Lieut. Colonels	16,757-03-04
Deputy Quarter-Master General	11,171-07-07
Brigade Majors, Captains, Surgeons, etc.	5,585-11-09
Lieutenants, 2d. Lieutenants, Asst. Surgeons	2,792-13-11
Conductors and Overseers	698-03-06
Sub-Conductors, Serjeant-Majors, Senior Serjeants	139-10-04
Serjeants	93-01-06
Corporals, Bombardiers, Gunners, Privates and Drummers	46-08-09

It may be noted that the distribution was not made until nearly 2 ½ years after the campaign! A Rupee in 1834 was the equivalent of two shillings (10 new pence).

It is sad to report that at the time of the Indian Mutiny, 'prize money' was simply loot and that cash, jewels, etc. were taken and often kept unreported by pillaging soldiers. Policing of this type of behaviour was particularly difficult and frequently went unpunished.

To obtain a more coherent picture – and, in some cases a more personal account of an action – the researcher is advised to seek published regimental histories or well researched accounts of specific actions.

Section 17 War Services

EIC Medal Rolls and Prize Rolls for Campaigns in India 1799 to 1861

IOR Reference	Medal Roll
L/MIL/5/42 – 44	EIC General Service Medal 1799 – 1826
L/MIL/5/45	EIC General Service Medal 1854
L/MIL/5/46 – 51	North-West Frontier 1849 – 1863 and Umbeyla 1863
L/MIL/5/52 – 54	Pegu 1852 – 1853
L/MIL/5/55 – 56	Persia 1856 – 1857
L/MIL/5/67	China 1842
L/MIL/5/68	Jellalabad (2nd Issue)
L/MIL/5/69	Scinde 1843
L/MIL/5/70	Sutlej 1845 – 1846
L/MIL/5/71 – 72	Punjab 1848 – 1849
L/MIL/5/73 – 105	Indian Mutiny 1857 – 1858
L/MIL/5/128 et seq	Miscellaneous 1845 –

Prize and Batta Rolls 1793 – 1858 *(a few minor campaigns have been omitted)*
(For explanation of 'Batta' see pages 12-13)

IOR Reference	Prize Roll
L/MIL/5/142 – 149	Dutch, French and Other Ships 1793 – 1811
L/MIL/5/150	Cochin, 1795
L/MIL/5/151 – 158	Ceylon, Amboyna and Banda, 1795 – 1796
L/MIL/5/159 – 160	Seringapatam, 1799; Hathras, 1817 (vol 160)
L/MIL/5/161 – 162	Egypt, 1801
L/MIL/5/164 – 165	Second Mahratta War, 1803 – 1805
L/MIL/5/166	Tranquebar, 1808
L/MIL/5/169 – 170	Ile de Bourbon, 1810
L/MIL/5/171 – 174	Mauritius, 1810
L/MIL/5/176 – 177	Ternate, 1810
L/MIL/5/175 – 183	Java, 1811
L/MIL/5/184 – 186	Palembang, 1812
L/MIL/5/187 – 243	Deccan, 1817 – 1819
L/MIL/5/245	Rassool Khyma, 1819-1820
L/MIL/5/247 – 252	Ava, 1824 – 1826
L/MIL/5/253 – 257	Bhurtpore, 1826
L/MIL/5/258	Coorg, 1834
L/MIL/5/259 – 261	First Afghan War, 1839 – 1842; Gwalior, 1843 (vol 261)
L/MIL/5/262 – 272	China 1840 – 1842
L/MIL/5/273	Nepaunee, 1841
L/MIL/5/274 – 275	Meeanee, Hyderabad and Sind, 1843
L/MIL/5/276	Indus, Sutlej & Punjab, 1846 – 1849
L/MIL/5/277 – 282	Burma (Pegu), 1852 – 1853
L/MIL/5/283 – 284	Persia, 1856 – 1857
L/MIL/5/285 – 290	Delhi
L/MIL/5/291 – 298	Lucknow, 1857 – 1858
L:/MIL/5/299 – 305	Banda and Kirwee, 1858
L/MIL/5/305 – 309	Jhansi
L/MIL/5/314	Other Mutiny Actions, 1857 – 1858

17.2 Printed Sources

Finally, from about the year:

Bombay – 1856	Madras – 1860	Bengal - 1865

the Annual Army List for the Presidency concerned records the 'War Service' of each officer. These records are provided for all officers still serving at the beginning of the year of the List. For officers this can be a convenient summary of the details that may be found as described in Section 8 above. Such information is not generally available for 'Other Ranks'. However, if, later in his career, an ordinary soldier ancestor was promoted to the ranks of Warrant Officer (sub-Conductor, or higher) in the Unattached List, he will, after all, have his 'War Service' recorded in the Army Lists.

As an example of this latter, I reproduce the 'War Service' of a Warrant Officer, taken at random from the January 1862 edition of 'The Madras Army List' (IOR Reference L/MIL/17/3/116), Conductor William Battison. Although 1862 follows the end of the East India Company's Armies, the services described occurred, of course, prior to their disbandment.

--ooOOoo--

Warrant Officers of the Commissariat Department

Conductor of Ordnance W. Battison was present at the capture of Rangoon on 11th May 1824, at the half-way stockade on advance to, and also of the Main, and at Kemmendine, 3d June 1824. At the attack and destruction of the seven stockades on 8th July 1824. Attack of the *Syrian* on 3d August 1824. At the siege and defence of the Shoe Dragon Pagoda from 1st to 12th, and at the attack and storming of the Kokeen Stockade on the 15th December 1824, proceeded to Pegu in November 1825 and accompanied the advance of Brigadier Pepper's force towards Shoay Gheen and Tonghoo – was present at the attack and capture of Shoay Gheen on 2d January 1826.

--ooOOoo--

Note that William Battison was a Bombardier in 2nd Battalion Madras Artillery at the time of these actions, having arrived in India aboard *Prince Regent* in 1822 (L/MIL/11/133). If he had not achieved Warrant Rank, it is probable that his war service would not be available.

17.3 Post-Mutiny Discharge Papers

As indicated in Section 13 above, each soldier opting for discharge rather than service in the British Army, following the Mutiny, was issued with a package of 'Discharge Papers'. These papers included some details of the participation of the soldier concerned in various military actions during his career. An example of this is reproduced on page 53.

18. Baptisms, Marriages and Burials

This section applies both to officers and soldiers.

Records of Baptism (sometimes of Birth), Marriage and Burial (sometimes of Death) are available from the following major sources:

18. 1. 'Ecclesiastical Returns'

It was Government policy in all three presidencies that all Baptisms, Marriages and Burials of Europeans in India be recorded by the Minister in the Church in which the ceremony was performed. Then, quarterly, the Minister was required to forward a certified copy of his registers to the Ecclesiastical authority in the presidency. These copies were collated and now reside at the IOR in London where some industrious worker has graciously provided annual alphabetical indexes to all records in all three presidencies. From the genealogical viewpoint, these are the most important and most frequently consulted records in the IOR. Indeed, from the information provided in these returns, the IOR is able to provide certificates of the event in question, legally valid, if needed, as for certificates provided by a Registrar in the U.K.

These records apply to all persons of European descent and most Christians of Anglo-Indian descent, and not only those of military personnel. The earliest records date from the end of the 17th century and stretch to Independence and beyond. Firstly, it is necessary to consult the Indexes. They are initially classified according to Presidency, viz:

> Bengal is Z/N/1   Madras is Z/N/2   Bombay is Z/N/3

These three Presidencies are the major areas into which these records are divided. Note that returns for Bengal cover the whole of northern India as well as the province of Bengal itself. For records of the 'other' areas under Company control please refer to the table on 'Regional Breakdown of Ecclesiastical Records' presented on page 73.

Then, for each presidency the indexes are broken down into Baptisms, Marriages and Burials. Next, each index is broken down into initial letter of the surname and then by year in which the event took place. Regrettably, although for many marriages the bride's name appears beside that of her husband in the indexes, the latter are not available alphabetically for the women. Lists indexed alphabetically by brides' names are, however, being made available from transcriptions made by volunteers and placed on various web-sites.

Note that some of the indexes provide references preceded by 'RC'. This means that the main entry is to be found in the series of Roman Catholic registers, which were separately kept as described on page 72. These records are separately indexed in LDS Film No. 527435 and the list of films of the records containing the full baptism, marriage and burial themselves can be accessed by typing this number into the 'FamilySearch' Film/Fiche Search function.

Others, in the Madras Presidency only, provide references preceded by either:

- 'O' – this refers to an 'omission' from the earlier index, or
- 'C' – this means that an earlier index error in the entry has been corrected

When the appropriate entry has been located, a Volume and Folio Number will be found alongside. These should be noted and combined with the presidency reference to give, for example for a <u>Madras</u> marriage of John Robert Roskell in 1856:

Roskell, John Robert to Emily Evans N/2/36 Fo.112 (N/2 for Madras/Volume 36, folio 112)

The registers themselves may be consulted on one of a series of corresponding microfilms located in cabinets in the IOR Reading Room.

The records themselves provide information such as one would expect, for example:

Marriages solemnized at: St. Thomas' Mount during the Quarter January to March 1856		
Date of Marriage:	15 January 1856	
Names of Parties - Christian:	John Robert	Emily
- Surname	Roskell	Evans
Ages of Parties	31	15
Condition	Bachelor	Spinster
Rank or Profession:	Laboratory Serjeant	-
Residence:	St. Thomas Mount	St.Thomas Mount
Name of Father:	George Roskell	Edward Evans
Licence or Banns:	By Licence	
Signature of Witnesses:	J. Battersby	Agnes Gibury
Ceremony performed by:	P. Gammon C.C.	

From 1835 (Madras Presidency) and 1842 (Bengal and Bombay Presidencies) Roman Catholic priests were appointed at the Company's expense, for the benefit of the rapidly increasing numbers of Roman Catholic soldiers in its armies, mostly of Irish origin. These priests were then required to make quarterly returns of Baptisms, Marriages and Burials in the same way as their Anglican brethren.

Until about 1854, these R.C. records were kept separate from the Anglican records, however, and are indexed under:

Bengal	N/1/RC/1-5	1842-1856
Madras	N/2/RC/1-7	1835-1845
	N/2/RC/8	1852-1854
Bombay	N/3/RC/1-5	1842-1854

After these dates, the Roman Catholic records should be found within the main indexes. It is unfortunate that the Madras records between 1845 and 1852 are missing.

It is sometimes estimated that the 'official' records of Baptism, Marriage and Burial are 80 percent complete. The author believes this figure to be significantly too high, since:

a. Births, Marriages and Deaths are also recorded in the East India Registers & Directories (1809-1842) and in the Almanacs of the individual presidencies from the early to mid 19th century. Comparisons of these records with those of the N/- series indicate that significant numbers of these events do not appear in the latter. It is, therefore, recommended that the East India Registers & Directories and Almanacs be researched if an event cannot be found in the N/- series – particularly if an officer is involved.

b. In the earlier days, the records covered only the Established Churches (Church of England and Church of Scotland). By the mid-1820s probably half of the soldier recruits to the Company's armies were Irishmen, almost all of them Roman Catholics. Copies of Registers of Catholic Churches were not required to be returned until 1835 (Madras) and 1842 (Bengal and Bombay). A very significant number of records taken prior to this date are thus excluded from the N/- series. It is also unfortunate that, even after these dates, Roman Catholic priests appear to have been less focussed on the need to adhere to this regulation and therefore many Roman Catholic ceremonies remained without return to the authorities.

c. Records for Burma were also supposed to have been returned to the Ecclesiastical authorities in Calcutta, before they were considered separately in 1937 (IOR series N/6). Possibly because of the relative difficulty of communication within that country, many records are believed to be missing. Many records from Malacca and Singapore were not copied to the authorities in India.

d. It should be remembered that large parts of the sub-continent were not directly under the Company's control. The map on the back cover of this book indicates the approximate division of the country between British India and the various independent Indian states in 1858, shortly before the end of the 'Company Era'. Unfortunately returns of Baptism, Marriage and Burial from the Indian states may not always have been made to the presidency authorities. For the years 1890-1945 returns from the Indian states may be found either in the three main presidency series or in a separate series (IOR N/5).

Further records are available for other areas under the control of the East India Company. These include the 'Indian States', St Helena, Fort Marlborough, Penang (Prince of Wales Island), Macao and Whampoa, Burma (separately treated 1937-1957), Kuwait and Aden. The following table indicates the availability of these records.

Regional Breakdown of Ecclesiastical Records

(Baptisms, Marriages and Burials)

Catalogue Section	Presidency or Region	Range of Volumes	Range of Years	LDS Film Range* (I = Index)
N/1	Bengal	1 – 641	1713 – 1948	498954 - 535699
		RC/1-5	1842 – 1844	527437
N/2	Madras	1 – 176	1698 – 1948	463296 - 527486
		RC/1-8	1835 – 1854	530008 - 530011
	Cochin	177	1751 – 1804	
N/3	Bombay	1 – 178	1709 – 1948	462965 - 523914
		RC/1-5	1842 – 1844	528361
N/4	India and Pakistan	1 – 8	1949 – 1968	527415 - 527421
N/5	Indian States	1 – 2	1890 – 1946	498603 (I) & 527422-3
N/6	St. Helena	1 – 3	1767 – 1835	498603 (I) & 498605
N/7	Fort Marlborough	1	1759 – 1825	498603 (I) & 498606
N/8	Penang (Prince of Wales Island)	1	1799 – 1829	498603 (I) & 498606
N/9	Macao & Whampoa	1	1820 – 1834	498603 (I) & 498606
N/10	Burma	1 – 7	1937 – 1957	527436 (I) & 534495
N/11	Registry Office Marriages	1 – 11	1852 – 1911	Not Filmed
N/12	Kuwait Political Agency	1 – 16	1937 – 1961	Not Filmed
N/13	Aden	1 – 21	1840 – 1969	Believed unfilmed
N/14	Register Lists (Registration Act 1886)			
		1	Bengal	
		2	Bombay	
		3	Madras, Assam, Burma, Central Provinces and Punjab	

*   or Film Numbers to insert into LDS Catalogue to yield full range.

Note: The LDS tend to classify the locations of these ecclesiastical events according to the present day Indian States, which the researcher will have to relate to the provinces of the former British Presidencies.

18.2 Transcriptions

Various individuals have made a number of transcriptions of Indian parish records. Generally, these have been deposited either with the IOR, or with the Society of Genealogists and a list of these latter is given on page 84.

Of particular interest to researchers of Roman Catholic soldier ancestors are the Baptismal records of both the Portuguese Mission church at St. Thomas' Mount, near Madras (1751 to 1880). This was the headquarters of the Madras Artillery and, therefore, features a large number of Irish Catholic soldiers who served in the Artillery in the years before 'emancipation' (1829). These records are not included in the IOR N/2 series but are on the shelves in the Reading Room. They are also available on the 'Families in British India Society' web-site at www.fibis.org.

Other transcriptions, which feature on this site, include those of large sections of the Marriage Indexes and smaller sections of the Baptism and Burial Indexes. The Marriage Indexes are particularly useful since they permit the relatively easy location by the name of the bride, formerly a laborious exercise.

18.3 Registry Office Marriages

From 1852, authority was given for the celebration of 'Registry Office Marriages'. The IOR hold records of these in their N/11 series. The indexes are contained in a volume Z/N/11 which is broken down into groups of years as follows:

N/11/1-3 (grouped together)	1852-1870
N/11/4	1871-1875
N/11/5	1876-1880
N/11/6	1881-1885
N/11/7	1886-1890
N/11/8	1891-1895
N/11/9 Part1	1896-1900 Nos. 1-694
N/11/9 Part2	1896-1900 Nos. 695-1413
N/11/10 Part 1	1901-1905 Nos. 1-514
N/11/10 Part 2	1901-1905 Nos. 515-1049
N/11/10 Part 3	1901-1905 Nos. 1050-1587
N/11/11	1906-1911

From 1886 (N/11/7 et seq.) the Deputy Registrar's District where the marriage took place is listed in the indexes. Prior to this date, only the name of the groom is listed alphabetically by surname, plus the name of his bride and the volume and folio number of the record itself.

18.4 LDS Microfilms

Luckily, for researchers less able to get to London, the LDS has microfilmed both the indexes and registers and makes them available at nominal charge at their Family History Centres. The number of films involved is very considerable. When printed out the lists of indexes and volumes themselves occupy 27 close-typed pages and so only the ranges of the films of the indexes are indicated below. It is, however, possible to examine them by visiting the LDS Catalogue of Microfilms on their web-site at: www.familysearch.org.

It is first necessary to search the Indexes. These Indexes are covered by:

Presidency-Ceremony	Years	Microfilm Range
Bengal Baptisms	1713 – 1948	0498511 to 0498531
Bengal Marriages	1713 – 1948	0498532 to 0498542
Bengal Burials	1713 – 1948	0498543 to 0498556
Bombay Baptisms	1709 – 1948	0498557 to 0498562
Bombay Marriages	1709 – 1948	0498563 to 0498566
Bombay Burials	1709 – 1948	0498567 to 0498573
Madras Baptisms	1698 – 1948	0498574 to 0498584
Madras Marriages	1698 – 1947	0498585 to 0498590
Madras Burials	1698 – 1947	0498591 to 0498600

It will be noticed that the film numbers are nicely in sequence throughout these indexes. However, interpolation is not advised since the split of years is not regular. It will be found helpful to enter into the LDS 'FamilySearch' Film/Fiche search section of their catalogue the film number at the beginning of the range of interest and then to select the film representing the correct combination of year and initial letter of surname sought.

Once the correct person has been identified, the reference to the volume and folio number of the record itself should be noted.

The search for Film numbers for the indexes within a given presidency will also provide the numbers for the films containing the full records themselves in that presidency. So, the above numbers may also be used to access the correct part of the 'FamilySearch' catalogue. It will be found that a given film in this section generally contains the baptisms, marriages and burials together for between three and six months for the presidency in question.

It should also be mentioned that the LDS have separately filmed certain of the entries of the original registers either in the original parish, or those sent to the local Bishop for safe keeping. These include many of the Roman Catholic parishes of the R.C. Diocese of Madras-Mylapore and of the parishes of the former Straits Settlements. These should be identified in the 'FamilySearch' catalogue directly by inserting the name of the state by which it is currently known. These records are not in the IOR.

18.5 Directories

'Announcements' of Births, Marriages and Deaths were frequently made in Directories of the day. These were similar to the practice today of making such announcements in national or local newspapers. Although these 'Domestic Occurrences', as they were termed, did not feature during the earlier years, the major Directories to which this applied were:

- **East India Register** (later East India Register & Directory) from 1809 to 1844. Here the announcements are reported by Presidency and by date. It should be mentioned that such announcements generally appear in the directory dated up to two years after the event in question.

- **Calcutta Annual Register & Directory (Bengal)** (1813 – 1858)

- **Madras Almanac** (1799 – 1861)

- **Bombay Almanac** (1806 – 1868)

Although these 'Domestic Occurrences' are useful in the absence of a corresponding entry in the N/ series records, the information that they contain is restricted according to the fashion of the time. For example, a birth may be recorded simply as:

On the 14th inst. to the lady of Captain Jones, 73rd Native Infantry, a son.

It is especially important to re-state that very many of these entries are not matched by a corresponding entry in the N/ series records. Accordingly, they represent a particularly valuable addition to the vital records available in British India.

19. Wills, Administrations, Probate and Estate Inventories

19.1 Separate Soldiers' and Officers' Wills Deposited in India

The following lists refer to the Wills of East India Company Soldiers, and of those of the Indian Army. They generally relate to those cases where they had little more to bequeath than their immediate personal effects. The LDS has not filmed these records. The ranges of years overlap, and therefore the final column gives the 'range of the majority' of wills

'Officers' Wills' are only 37 in number and, being so few, they are considered as an adjunct to 'Soldiers' Wills'. Those included apply to all three presidencies and cover April 1831 to July 1875. These are included in IOR reference: L/AG/34/30/30.

Soldiers' Wills

	Reference	Vol No.	Years Covered	Range of Majority
Bengal	L/AG/34/30/1	1	1825 – 1840	1838 – 1839
	L/AG/34/30/2	2	1825 – 1841	1839 – 1841
	L/AG/34/30/3	3	1833 – 1843	1841 – 1843
	L/AG/34/30/4	4	1825 – 1845	1843 – 1844
	L/AG/34/30/5	5	1833 – 1846	1845 – 1846
	L/AG/34/30/6	6	1839 – 1848	1846 – 1848
	L/AG/34/30/7	7	1833 – 1861	1848 – 1849
	L/AG/34/30/8	8	1837 – 1851	1848 – 1851
	L/AG/34/30/9	9	1838 – 1853	1850 – 1852
	L/AG/34/30/10	10	1841 – 1854	1852 – 1853
	L/AG/34/30/11	11	1846 – 1856	1853 – 1855
	L/AG/34/30/12	12	1845 – 1857	1855 – 1857
Madras	L/AG/34/30/13	1	1825 – 1841	1838 – 1840
	L/AG/34/30/14	2	1834 – 1842	1841 – 1842
	L/AG/34/30/15	3	1824 – 1846	1843 – 1845
	L/AG/34/30/16	4	1837 – 1848	1846 – 1847
	L/AG/34/30/17	5	1840 – 1851	1848 – 1850
	L/AG/34/30/18	6	1836 – 1853	1851 – 1853
	L/AG/34/30/19	7	1839 – 1856	1853 – 1855
	L/AG/34/30/20	8	1847 – 1858	1855 – 1858
	L/AG/34/30/21	9	1852 – 1863	1858 – 1862
	L/AG/34/30/22	10	1844 – 1881	1863 – 1881
Bombay	L/AG/34/30/23	1	1825 – 1842	1839 – 1842
	L/AG/34/30/24	2	1838 – 1844	1842 – 1844
	L/AG/34/30/25	3	1820 – 1846	1844 – 1846
	L/AG/34/30/26	4	1839 – 1852	1846 – 1852
	L/AG/34/30/27	5	1826 – 1856	1850 – 1855
	L/AG/34/30/28	6	1853 – 1860	1855 – 1859
	L/AG/34/30/29	7	1857 – 1868	1859 – 1862

19.2 Wills Deposited in General Jurisdictions

Wills of many officers and a small number of soldiers may be found in one of a number of locations. Many are outside India and include most or all the standard locations in the United Kingdom. This assumes that the officer deposited one before proceeding to India or whilst at home on furlough. By about 1727, the Company authorities in India were granted the power to act in the matter of probate and the administration of property of Europeans living in India. Naturally this covered all such citizens, not only civilians but also the officers and soldiers of the East India Company's Armies. So, many Wills, Probates and Administrations may be found in the court records of the presidency of the soldier's service. It is thus appropriate to include these more general records in this work.

These records are sometimes included together, sometimes separately and sometimes in various combinations. It is our purpose here to indicate the existence of such records and to guide the researcher towards them. However, in view of their diversity and plurality, we indicate the major indexes and the records, which they summarize. This should be adequate for all but the advanced researcher. Otherwise, we advise a visit to the IOR, to consult their catalogues, or the viewing of the major films of indexes at the LDS Family History Centres.

Wills were proven, Administrations granted and Inventories lodged in the various courts established for general adjudication in each presidency. In summary, these were:

Early Courts of Justice operating in

      Bengal (1704-1774)   Madras (1753-1797)   Bombay (1704-1798).

Supreme or Recorders' Courts operating in

      Calcutta (1774-1862)   Madras (1797-1862)   Bombay (1798-1862)

High Courts operating in

      Calcutta (1862-1948)   Madras (1862-1948)   Bombay (1862-1948)

District Courts, and High Courts and Chief Courts, other than those in the presidency seats of government, established in major cities in each presidency to supplement the latter. These were established at various times after 1865.

The 'Will Records' may be broken down into both Indexes and the Wills themselves. As always, it is important to consult the indexes first in any of the series. Please note that the records are inconsistent across the presidencies, across the years and in the descriptions of what they contain. It may be remarked that it has been less straightforward in this instance to provide a one-to-one correspondence between the IOR Catalogue numbers and the LDS Film Numbers. Accordingly, the records are separately classified and presented in the two tables on page 80. Researchers constrained to use the LDS Film series are once more advised to insert the 'Suggested Film No.' into the LDS on-line catalogue. This will yield the complete list of films in the series in question. The catalogue numbers (IOR series) are provided in condensed format but the full series may, of course, be viewed in the IOR Reading Room catalogues.

19.3 Military Estate Papers and Treasury Deposits

Neither of these two sets of records has been filmed by the LDS, although the indexes to Treasury Deposits have and may be found in the tables below. The records apply both to Officers and other ranks of the Company's Armies and Indian Armies and extend from 1792 to 1927 (Treasury Deposits) and 1849 to 1937 (Military Estate Papers). There are no indexes to the Military Estate Papers available in the IOR but those to the Treasury Deposits may be used, since for each entry in the latter, there is generally a corresponding entry in the former.

Inventories, Wills Administration and Probate

A. General Wills and Administrations Index (1780-1938)

		IOR References	LDS Film No.
Bengal	General Administrations Index	Z/L/AG/34/4-5	507804 & 2046671
Bengal	General Wills Index	Z/L/AG/34/6-7	507804 & 2046671
Madras	General Wills and Admons Index	Z/L/AG/34/8	2046671
Bombay	General Wills and Admons Index	Z/L/AG/34/10	2046671

B. Early Court Records for all three presidencies:

Bengal 1704 – 1774   **Madras** 1753 – 1779   **Bombay** 1704 – 1783

Index or Series.	IOR Ref:	LDS Film No
Index	Z/L/AG/34/1 – 2	510705
IOR Series	P/1/1-6, P/154/40-55	506793* (Bengal)
	and P/155/9-38	523815* (Madras)
		523819* (Bombay)

C. Records of Supreme or Recorders' Courts (prior to 1862) and High Courts of Calcutta, Madras and Bombay (from 1862 to 1937)

Presidency/Date Range	Index or Series	IOR Reference	LDS Film No.
Calcutta 1774 – 1862	Index	Z/L/AG/34/6 – 7	507804
	IOR Series	L/AG/34/29/1 – 184	507805*
Madras 1780 – 1862	Index	Z/L/AG/34/9	506881
	IOR Series	L/AG/34/29/185-340	506882*
Bombay 1783 – 1862	Index	Z/L/AG/34/10	2046671
	IOR Series	L/AG/34/29/341-381	506936*

D. Records of District Courts (i.e. High Courts and Chief Courts other than those of Calcutta, Madras and Bombay, established at various dates after 1865)

Index or Series	IOR Reference	LDS Film No.
Index	Z/L/AG/34/12	
IOR Series	L/AG/34/31/1-21 Believed Unfilmed	
Calendars of Probate	L/AG/34/12/1-12 530013*	

* Suggested Film No. to insert into LDS Catalogue search

LDS Films of Indexes to Wills, Admons, Probates, Military Estates, Inventories and Treasury Deposits

LDS Film No.	Contents
2046652	Indexes to Wills and Administrations 1618 to 1779
	Index to Inventories, etc. 1753 to 1779
	Index to Administrations 1774 to 1888
2046671	Index to Administrations, Bengal 1889 to 1909
	Index to Administrations, Madras 1780 to 1909
	Index to Wills, Madras 1780 to 1908
	Index to Wills and Administrations, Bombay 1776 to 1909
	Index to Wills and Administrations, Bengal (natives) 1890 to 1900
	Index to Calendars granted by District Courts, 1865 to 1910
	Index to Inventories and Accounts Current, 1780 to 1909
2046672	Index to Inventories, Madras 1780 to 1909
	Index to Inventories, Bombay 1778 to 1910
	Index to Treasury Deposits, Bengal 1792 to 1919
	Index to Treasury Deposits, Madras 1806 to 1896
2046673	Index to Treasury Deposits, Bombay 1822 to 1895
	Index to Estates advertised by Administrators General, 1877 to 1911
	Index to Wills, Administrations, Inventories and Accounts, Straits Settlements 1728 to 1853
	Index to Wills, Administrations, Inventories and Accounts, St. Helena 1705 to 1836

Note that these films refer to a recently compiled Summary Index of Wills now available on the open shelves in the IOR Reading Room and containing: Z/L/AG/34/1 to 12.

Also included are Indexes to Treasury Deposits Z/L/AG/34/17 to 21, as follows:

Z/L/AG/34/17	Bengal 1792-1888	Z/L/AG/34/19	Madras 1806-1859
Z/L/AG/34/18	Bengal 1889-1919 plus	Z/L/AG/34/20	Madras 1856-1894
	All India 1894-1919	Z/L/AG/34/21	Bombay 1824-1895

Note that these may be used as a guide index to the Military Estate Papers.

Earlier filming of Indexes to Wills and Administrations are:

506881 Item 1	Index to Madras Wills 1708 to 1908
506881 Item 2	Index to Madras Administrations 1780 to 1908
506881 Item 3	List of Wills found in Bengal Public Consultations (Vols. I to VI)
510705	Index to Wills and Administrations, Bengal 1710 to 1779
510705	Index to Wills and Administrations, Madras 1736 to 1779
510705	Index to Wills and Administrations, Bombay 1723 to 1775

20. Further Sources

Almost all the records cited above may be classed as 'standard' records. Indeed, they are all essentially lists in which a researcher's ancestor may feature. There are, however, many types of record in which he may feature, which may be classed as non-standard or in which he may be found in isolation from his colleagues. Such records include:-

20.1 General Orders

Each presidency authority issued 'orders' or regulations on a very regular basis. They were generally later compiled into printed volumes and issued annually. Many of these 'orders' were instructions to named individuals to undertake a specific duty such as:

- Detachment to special duties
- Authority to proceed on furlough or sick leave
- Appointments to the Board of a Court Martial
- Confirmation of Discharge to Pension
- Promotions
- Etc.

They are to be found in:-

Presidency	Title	Date Range	IOR Reference Range
Bengal	Standing General Orders by C-in-C	1820-1861*	L/MIL/17/2/269-352
Madras	General Orders	1800-1817	L/MIL/17/3/335-370
	General Orders by Government	1816-1895	L/MIL/17/3/371-411
	General Orders by C-in-C	1818-1860*	L/MIL/17/3/412-426
Bombay	Standing General Orders by C-in-C	1820-1861	L/MIL/17/4/363-390
	General Orders by Governor-in-Council and C-in-C	1842-1860*	L/MIL/17/4/412-430
	General Orders by C-in-C	1856-1860	L/MIL/17/4/465-467

*Series continues beyond Company era.

As one might expect, officers feature highly, as also do Surgeons and Apothecaries, especially with respect to their appointments to various regiments or stations. Nevertheless, 'Other Ranks' feature in special circumstances and their mention may throw some light on the background to their lives. Of particular interest are the summary reports of the proceedings of courts martial. They provide full details of the accused, of the date and place of the alleged crime, names of others involved plus the verdict and punishment, if appropriate. Many details of soldiers may be found here which do not feature in other records.

Furthermore, it was practice for soldiers to entrust their 'savings' to their superior officer, or the adjutant of their various corps. Such transactions are often recorded in the General or Standing Orders and generally give at least the name of the Company to which the donor was attached and the name of his superior officer.

None of these records has been filmed by the LDS and, unfortunately, there are no indexes to them before about the middle of the 1840's. This makes their consultation very time-consuming. However, no study should be considered complete without reference to them.

20.2 Military Proceedings

Each presidency government department, and from 1834 the Government of India, issued minutes of its 'Proceedings' (IOR series 'P'). These departments were variously styled:

Bengal: 'Military Department' or 'Secret and Military Department'

Madras: 'Military Department', 'Military and Secret Department' or 'Military and Political Department'

Bombay: 'Military Department'

Such proceedings are very wide in scope but occasionally refer to individual officers or soldiers. They are indexed but not in a helpful fashion and browsing can be laborious. However, the earlier records date from the mid eighteenth century and may contain information not available elsewhere. Examples of the data they contain include confirmation of application for pensions by widows.

Although not high on the list of priorities for researchers, if the individual sought is, indeed, found in these records the researcher will consider himself adequately rewarded.

20.3 Military Correspondence

The type of documentation described in this section normally focuses on a campaign, battle, or other military activity, rather than on the individual officers and soldiers who happened to be participants in it. A list of the major wars and battles involving the Company's – and British – Armies in India is given in Table 2. It may require considerable research to locate material on the action in which your ancestor was involved, and even then he may not be mentioned by name unless he took a particularly prominent part in it. For example, reference is frequently made to the participation of a 'company of the Bengal European Regiment' or 'a detachment of Madras Artillery' without mention of the specific unit involved, let alone the name of the officer commanding it. Officers are more likely to be referred to than soldiers, but if one of the latter particularly distinguished himself he may get a 'mention in despatches'. However, for those wishing to explore the possibility of finding a reference to their ancestor 'in action' the following information may be of use when starting out.

From its earliest days the East India Company's Court of Directors in London conducted an increasingly voluminous correspondence with its servants in India, copies of which are to be found principally in three IOR series: E/4, F/4, and (for military matters) L/MIL/3.

The E/4 series contains the Company's copies of its letters from and despatches to the three Presidencies (and also from 1834 the Government of India). The correspondence covers a wide range of subjects, including military but excluding secret matters. There are indexes (Z/E/4) for the years 1753-1858, all of which are available in the IOR Reading Room except those for pre-1801 Bengal which have to be ordered. The indexes give references only to the outward despatches from London, but since an outward despatch will usually refer to an inward letter on the same topic and give its date, it is possible to use them to find letters from India, albeit in a roundabout way. Enclosures to the letters from India may often be as important as the despatch itself, but unfortunately these are not usually present in E/4 and have to be located in the L/MIL/3 series (see next paragraph). The E/4 series ends with the demise of the Company.

The Board of Control, as part of its responsibility to supervise the Company's activities on behalf of the Government, also kept copies of the Company's correspondence, and the military letters and despatches are in the L/MIL/3 series which runs from 1803 to well into the twentieth century. (It also includes a second set of the outward despatches acquired from the Company when it was abolished). Unfortunately this series has no modern index. On the other hand it usefully separates the military correspondence from the rest, and more importantly, it does contain the enclosures to letters from India (sometimes bound separately). If, therefore, you know the date of the letter you are looking for, it may offer a quicker route to finding it than E/4, and it is the only route to finding the enclosures. In sum the two series E/4 and L/MIL/3 need to be used in conjunction with each other.

Finally, as part of the process of seeking Government approval for a despatch, the Company had to submit to the Board of Control a collection of papers providing background information on the subject of that despatch. These 'Board's Collections' as they are known are in F/4, they are dated 1796 to 1858, and a modern index up to 1845 is available in the IOR Reading Room. If you are lucky enough to locate a Board's Collection on the military subject you are interested in, you will find that the clerks of East India House have assembled most of the relevant papers for you (including copies of letters and despatches).

20.4 'Soldiers' References' 1860 - 1873

These are a series of correspondence, and registers of correspondence, received by the Company and India Office Military Departments from soldiers and their relatives. They include enquiries about the whereabouts of soldiers, applications for medals, prize money, allowances etc. They include tens of thousands of sets of correspondence contained in references L/MIL/5/362-375 and there are registers in Z/L/MIL/5/16-43.

It may be added here that the L/MIL/5 series contains many more files that may contain data of varying genealogical value. However, they are only available to visitors to the India Office Records.

20.5 The British Association for Cemeteries in South Asia (BACSA)

This organization has assumed the daunting task of organizing the maintenance and preservation of graves in South Asia. During the course of their activity, they have produced a series of books listing large numbers of graves and transcribing their inscriptions. BACSA is understood currently to be preparing to list much of their data on their website at: www.bacsa.org.uk. In the meantime, their publications are available in the India Office

Records at the British Library or may be purchased from BACSA at No 76½ Chartfield Avenue, London SW15 6HQ

20.6 National Army Museum

As well as the very important Hodson biographical card collection of officers of the Company's armies referred to on page 29, the NAM holds a significant number of private papers. These are similar in character to the India Office Private Papers (below) and, like them, are far more numerous for officers than for soldiers. The museum also has a strong collection of pictures, photographs, descriptions of uniforms, copies of regulations, etc. which provide useful background to the life of soldiers in India.

20.7 The Royal Artillery Library and Archive

The Library of the Museum of Artillery, ('Firepower' Museum) on the site of the former Royal Arsenal at Woolwich, contains a number of documents directly related not only to the Royal Artillery in India, but also to its predecessors, the various presidency armies of the Company. In particular, they hold some copies of Standing Orders of the three presidency Artillery Corps, not available in the IOR

20.8 The Society of Genealogists

At their Library at 14, Charterhouse Buildings, Goswell Rd, London EC1M 7BA, The Society of Genealogists has an extensive and valuable number of shelves devoted to the history of British India with, naturally, significant genealogical content. Their holdings are summarized in their publication entitled '*Sources for Anglo-Indian Genealogy in the Library of the Society of Genealogists*', published by Neville C. Taylor in 1990. Note that, in this context, Anglo-Indian means British persons in India. A list of the major sources of 'Vital Records' taken from this publication is presented in the table on the next page.

Among the more important items in their holdings is the The Society's India Card List. At the outbreak of World War II in 1939, Lieut. Col. H. K. Percy-Smith, one time Honorary Librarian of the Society of Genealogists in London, was re-called to duty in India. During his spare time there he produced a very extensive card index containing, in alphabetical order, the names of a wide variety of Europeans living in British India between 1785 to 1926. Each card provides the name of the individual, the date of an event in his/her life and a reference to the source from which it came. Evidently, many of the data are taken from more conventional sources in the India Office Records and elsewhere. However, many of the data are monumental inscriptions taken from the collections made by Lt. Col., later Brigadier, H. Bullock.

This index may be viewed at the Society's library, or on a range of LDS microfilms. The list of these film numbers is not sequential and so it is recommended that the researcher type in the number of the first film: 2220331 into the LDS' 'FamilySearch' catalogue. This will bring up the whole range of films with the various surname breaks.

Parish Records of Christenings, Marriage and Burials at the Society of Genealogists

Parish	Christenings	Marriages	Burials
Amritsar	1878 – 1946	1853 - 1944	
Dalhousie	1862 – 1935	1865 – 1942	
Delhi, St. Mary (R.C.)		1861 – 1913*	1872 – 1944
Gurdaspur	1870 – 1930	1871 – 1945*	1883 – 1943
Kalka	1901 – 1943	1921 – 1942	1843 – 1945
Kasauli	1845 – 1919*	1857 – 1919	1838 – 1945
Simla	1838-1865/1865-1914*	1838-1894/1895-1921*	1888 – 1945
Jutogh (near Simla)			
Simla (Christchurch)	1841 – 1901*	1895 – 1944	1892 – 1962
Coorg (Christchurch, Polibetta)			
Dalhousie	1897 – 1935	1838 – 1894	1810 – 1855
Benares, St. Mary	1810 – 1854	1810 – 1840	
Sanawar (near Kussowlee)		1849 – 1948	1849 – 1941
Srinagar	1863 – 1941	1876 – 1941	
Ootacamund		1831 – 1866	
St. Thomas' Mount (Portuguese Mission)	1751 - 1880		
Marriages in the Presidency of Fort St. George (Ed. H. Dodwell)		1680 – 1800	1713 – 1788
Bengal Par. Regs. (Bengal Past & Present)	1713 – 1788	1713 – 1792	1680 – 1746
Burials at Madras (Rev. C.H. Malden)			1826 – 1980
Register of European Deaths and Burials in Burma (R.E. McGuire)			

* = Extracts Only

The Society's collections include very many further lists, directories and other records relating to British India in general. Evidently, many of these include data relevant to military personnel of the East India Company's Armies.

20.9 The National Archives

Reference has already been made to the War Office Records (WO Series), which reside in The National Archive's collection at Kew. These include, in particular, the pension payments to retired soldiers of the Company's Armies in Europe. Furthermore, a number of soldiers transferred from the British Army to one of the Company's armies or from the Company's Armies to the British Army. Records of their service during their time with the British Army may be found at TNA in Kew.

A particular series of records, which has somehow found its way to Kew, is a partial list of the soldiers of the 4th Battalion, Madras Artillery. This may be found under their reference WO97 piece no. 1209. It has been filmed by the LDS (Film No. 861872) and includes a short summary of each soldier, including field service where appropriate.

20.10 The India Office Private Papers

The India Office Private Papers (formerly 'European Manuscripts') section at the British Library holds unpublished memoirs, diaries and letters of Europeans in India, including those who served in the East India Company's armies, deposited by officers, soldiers and their relatives. Inevitably there is a wealth of material from officers but rather little from the rank and file. A computer catalogue of these papers, indexed by name and subject, is available in the IOR Reading Room and on the web at www.bl.uk/catalogues/indiaofficeselect.

Documents such as these can be particularly helpful in the provision of background to the lives of personnel who served in the Company's armies. Although it is most unlikely that a researcher will find a document written by his ancestor, even if an officer, the chances are somewhat higher that the collection will contain one written by an ancestor's colleague and therefore indicate some of their common background.

Descriptions of life for the average East India Company Army officer in India are also to be found in the memoirs or diaries of serving officers. In fact, many researchers have used these and similar sources in combination with the excellent synopses to be found in the series described in Section 8 above, as a background to biographies of their ancestors. It is not really the purpose of this guide to recommend any particular book on the subject, although the author was impressed by the detail provided by *The Diary of an Indian Cavalry Officer* edited by Richard Morgan. These diaries cover the period from 1843 to 1863 and, therefore, give both a view of this officer's life in India in general, plus his particular experiences throughout the Indian Mutiny.

The nature of the average soldier's life is more difficult to determine and generally requires research and amalgamation of details extracted from the letters, diaries etc. of several individuals. Among the best single diary of these is the *Autobiography of David Dinwiddie* published in three parts, the Spring and Autumn 2003 plus the Summer 2004 editions of the *Journal of the Families in British India Society*. This was authorised by Brian Duncan and transcribed by Ruth Croft.

21. So, Where Do I Start?

Many researchers come to learn that their ancestor served in the army in India. Many have no idea in which army, where, when or in what capacity he served. It is first necessary to understand that there were the four major armies in which he could have served and that one should first determine in which one he did so.

Generally, the following rules apply.

1. An officer or soldier is frequently linked to his rank and to his regiment. Any regiment prefaced with the term His (or Her) Majesty's is a regiment of the British Army.

2. The various fighting corps of the East India Company are generally prefaced with the name of the presidency to which the army of that given corps was part. For example: First Bombay European Regiment, or Second Bengal Native Cavalry or Twenty-second Madras Native Infantry. Note that the latter is very frequently and typically abbreviated to 22nd M.N.I.

3. Private soldiers of a native regiment but with a European name were almost certainly of Anglo-Indian descent and not of fully European descent.

4. All soldiers of European regiments were of fully European descent. A few exceptions were sometimes possible in the case of Drummers, Buglers and Fifers.

5. Medical Officers (Surgeons and Assistant Surgeons), who were always Europeans, almost always formed part of the Company's military establishment and were allocated to regiments of both the British Army and Company's Army regiments on a temporary basis. The same applied to Apothecaries and Assistant Apothecaries, who were frequently either Europeans born in India, or Anglo-Indians.

Officers are almost always to be mentioned in the Army List of the presidency in which their regiments were serving (see section 8.5). This applied both to regiments of the British Army and of the Company's Army of that presidency. Generally, these regimental lists are repeated in the various Almanacs of the presidency concerned up to the demise of the Company's armies in about 1860. All officers are therefore relatively easy to locate and identify. Careers of officers of the British Army may then be pursued in the records at The National Archives at Kew.

Soldiers of the rank and file pose more of a problem. Any knowledge of their location at a particular date should help one to identify in which regiment they served. This would be through a combination of a knowledge of which regiments were serving at that location at the time and the Muster Lists of either the British Army or of the relevant presidency army. Once identified, the man's career may be followed backwards and forwards with the help of the Muster Lists and other records featured in this Guide.

Although strictly beyond the scope of this book, it will frequently be found that an officer or soldier who is identified as serving in the Indian Army after 1860, previously served in one of the Company's armies before, or at the time of the mutiny. In such cases, your man's career may be sought backwards by reference to the various records presented in this guide.

22. Results – One in Two Hundred Thousand

As pointed out in the previous section, the services of officers are given, at least in summary form, in the records described in section 8 of this Guide. However, those of 'Other Ranks' may well have to be compiled from a piecing together of the many disparate sources scattered through the India Office Records and/or by consultation of many of the LDS' films.

The standards of 'proof' required to establish genealogical and biographical precision require corroboration of all these disparate sources. It is necessary to ensure that a particular John Smith is the same John Smith all the way through a biographical project. A soldier is usually labelled with a regimental number or, in the case of a soldier of the East India Company Army, with the name of the ship and year of his arrival. This helps to avoid confusion. Even so, it is perhaps pertinent to point out that *EICS Minerva* carried three recruits to Madras in 1827 each with the name Michael McMahon! The researcher is advised to be wary of confusion and not to abandon good genealogical practice.

The list on the next two pages provides an example, with relevant references to the sources used, of just one of the estimated 200,000 soldiers who served in the Company's armies. It is typical, yet none is typical. However, by presenting this example, I hope to show the detail that can be achieved with perseverance.

Let us hope that your researches are similarly rewarded – Good Hunting!

Curriculum Vitae of Edward Evans of the Madras Army (author's ancestor)

Date	Age	Event	Rank - Unit	Location	Reference
24 Feb 1811	0	Birth		Lewisham, Kent	Baptism Entry, St. Mary's,
24 Mar 1811	0	Baptism		Lewisham, Kent	Baptism Entry, St. Mary's,
03 Oct 1828	17	Enlisted in HEIC Army	Silversmith	Manchester, Lancs.	L/MIL/9/9
06 Oct 1828	17	Attested for HEIC Army	Recruit- (Infantry)	Manchester, Lancs.	L/MIL/9/9
23 Oct 1828	17	Final Approval for Service	Recruit- (Infantry)	Chatham, Kent	L/MIL/9/9
06 Mar 1829	18	Embarked in HEICS *Thames*	Infantryman	Gravesend, Kent	L/MIL/9/77 and 100
17 Jun 1829	18	Disembarked at Madras	Infantryman	Fort St. George, Ma	L/MAR/B/8S
01 Jan 1830	18	Annual Muster	Gunner- 3d Batt. Art.	St. Thomas' Mount	L/MIL/11/136
01 Jan 1837	25	Annual Muster	Gunner- 3d Bn. Art.	St. Thomas' Mount	L/MIL/11/143
17 Oct 1837	26	Promotion (temporary) Corporal – 'C' Co. 3. Bn. Art. to Sjt. Major 14th N.I.		St. Thomas' Mount	L/MIL/17/3/417 Order 302
01 Dec 1837	26	Promotion to Laboratory Man		St. Thomas' Mount	L/MIL/17/3/417 Order 320
01 Jan 1839	27	Annual Muster	Laboratory Man	St. Thomas' Mount	L/MIL/11/145
14 Feb 1839	28	Promotion to Laboratory Corporal		St. Thomas' Mount	L/MIL/17/3/418 Order 57
1839	28	Married Teresa Ross		St. Mary's Cathedral	Deduction.
07 Sep 1839	28	Promotion to Serjeant Instructor		St. Thomas' Mount	L/MIL/17/3/418 Order 289
03 Aug 1840	29	Birth of Daughter, Emily	Serjeant Instructor	St. Thomas' Mount	St. Patrick's Parish Records and N/2/RC4 fo. 241
05 Sep 1841	30	Birth of Daughter, Catharine	Serjeant Instructor	St. Thomas' Mount	St. Patrick's Parish Records and N/2/RC1 fo.198
20 Oct 1841	30	Death of Wife, Teresa	Serjeant Instructor	St. Thomas' Mount	St. Mary's Cathedral Burials
01 Jan 1843	31	Annual Muster	Serjeant Instructor	St. Thomas' Mount	L/MIL/11/150
08 Feb 1843	31	Married Catherine Evers	Serjeant Instructor	St. Thomas' Mount	St. Patrick's Marr. Record and N/2/RC5 fo338
11 Apr 1844	33	Promotion to Laboratory Serjeant		St. Thomas' Mount	L/MIL/17/3/420 Order 148
17 Oct 1844	33	Birth of Son, William Peter	Laboratory Serjeant	St. Thomas' Mount	St. Patrick's Baptism Record and N/2/RC7 fo. 67

Curriculum Vitae of Edward Evans of the Madras Army (Continued)

Date	Age	Event	Rank - Unit	Location	Reference
10 Sep 1846	35	Birth of Daughter, Mary	Laboratory Serjeant	St. Thomas' Mount	St. Patrick's Baptism Records
1847	36	Illustrations for Artillery Book	Laboratory Serjeant	St. Thomas' Mount	'Instructions in Repository ....', IOR/T 35146
24 Feb 1849	38	Birth of Daughter, Anne	Laboratory Serjeant	St. Thomas' Mount	St. Patrick's Baptism Records
Mar 1851	40	Promoted Acting Sub-Conductor		St. Thomas' Mount	L/MIL/17/3/423 – Index only
15 Aug 1851	40	Birth of ds. Jane and Elizabeth	Actg. Sub-Conductor	St. Thomas' Mount	St. Patrick's Baptism Records
27 Feb 1852	51	Promotion to Sub-Conductor		St. Thomas' Mount	L/MIL/17/3/423 and L/MIL/11/101
20 Feb 1854	43	Birth of Daughter, Ellen	Sub-Conductor	St. Thomas' Mount	St. Patrick's Baptism Records and N/2/33 fo. 476
18 May 1855	44	Marriage of dau. Catherine	Sub-Conductor	St. Thomas' Mount	St. Patrick's Marriage Records
15 Jan 1856	44	Marriage of dau. Emily	Sub-Conductor	St. Thomas' Mount	St. Patrick's Marriage Records
19 Sep 1856	45	Birth of Daughter, Lucy	Sub-Conductor	St. Thomas' Mount	St. Patrick's Baptism Records and N/2/37 fo. 247
06 Mar 1858	47	Promotion to Conductor		St. Thomas' Mount	L/MIL/17/3/426 Page 307
01 Jan 1862	50	Annual Muster	Conductor	St. Thomas' Mount	Madras Army List & Almanac
15 Nov 1862	51	Transfer to Fort St. George	Conductor	Fort St. George	L/MIL/17/3/427 Page 626
01 Jan 1863	51	Annual Muster	Conductor	Fort St. George	Madras Army List & Almanac
31 Mar 1863	52	Pensioned	Pensioned Conductor	Madras	L/MIL/17/3/428 and L/MIL/11/98
1865	52	Secretary to Officers' Pension Committee		St. Thomas' Mount	Madras Almanac
April 1866	55	Letter to Daughter Emily's Father-in-law	Pensioned Conductor	Fort St. George	India Office Private Papers Mss Eur Photo Eur 479
01 Jan 1867	55	Annual Muster	Pensioned Conductor	Madras	L/MIL/11/190
28 Feb 1867	56	'In Memoriam' Published	Pensioned Conductor	St. Thomas' Mount	Book – IOR P/T 4222
20 Aug 1872	61	Died of 'Dysentry'	Pensioned Conductor	Madras	L/MIL/11/196 and N/2/53 fo. 205

Sacred to the Memory of Edward Paul Evans, Pensioned Conductor, Madras Ordnance Dept. Born 24 February 1811, Died 20 August 1872. For more than a quarter of a century clerk to the Retiring Fund of the Officers of the Madras Artillery by whom this tomb is erected as a token of respect and esteem for a faithful servant and deserving soldier. R.I.P. (From Edward's tombstone in St. Patrick's Cemetery in Madras).

Table 1 - Chronology of major EIC Acquisitions in India and the East

Year	Region Acquired	Presidency	Acquired From
1757	24 Parganas	Bengal	Nawab of Bengal
1759	Masulipatam	Madras	Nizam of Hyderabad
1760	Burdwan, Midnapore, Chittagong	Bengal	Nawab of Bengal
1765	Bengal, Bihar and Orissa	Bengal	Mogul Emperor
1765	Company *Jagir* in Madras	Madras	Nawab of Carnatic
1766	Northern Circars	Madras	Nizam of Hyderabad
1775	Zamindari of Benares	Bengal	Nawab of Oudh
1776	Island of Salsette	Bombay	Marathas
1778	Nagore	Madras	Raja of Tanjore
1778	Guntur Circar	Madras	Nizam of Hyderabad
1786	Penang	Bengal	Sultan of Kedah
1792	Malabar, Dindigul, Salem, etc	Madras	Sultan of Mysore
1799	Coimbatore, Kanara, Wynaad, etc	Madras	Sultan of Mysore
1799	Tanjore	Madras	Raja of Tanjore
1800	Nizam's districts of Mysore	Madras	Nizam of Hyderabad
1800	Province Wellesley	Bengal	Sultan of Kedah
1801	Carnatic	Madras	Nawab of Carnatic
1801	Gorakhpur, Lower Doab, Bareilly	Bengal	Nawab of Oudh
1802	Bundelkhand	Bengal	Peshwa
1803	Cuttack and Balasore	Madras	Raja of Nagpur
1803	Upper Doab, Delhi Territory	Bengal	Daulat Rao Scindia
1805	Gujarat	Bombay	Gaekwar of Baroda
1815	Kumaon and part of Terai	Bengal	Nepal
1817	Saugor, Hatta, Dharwar	Bombay	Peshwa
1817	Ahmadabad	Bombay	Gaekwar of Baroda
1818	Khandesh	Bombay	Holkar of Indore
1818	Ajmer	Bengal	Daulat Rao Scindia
1818	Poona, Konkan, South Maratha Ctry	Bombay	Peshwa
1818	Nerbudda, Sambalpur	Bengal	Raja of Nagpur
1819	Singapore (cession 1824)	Bengal	Sultan of Johore
1820	Southern Konkan	Bombay	Raja of Suwunt Waree
1822	Bijapur and Ahmadnagar	Bombay	Nizam of Hyderabad
1824	Singapore	Bengal	Sultan of Johore
1825	Malacca	Bengal	Netherlands
1826	Assam, Arakan, Tavoy, Tenasserim	Bengal	King of Ava
1834	Coorg	Madras	Raja of Coorg
1839	Aden	Bombay	Sultan of Aden
1843	Sind	Bombay	Amirs of Sind
1846/1849	Punjab	Bengal	Duleep Singh
1848	Satara*	Bombay	Raja of Satara (death of)
1849	Sambalpur*	Bengal	Raja of Sambalpur (death of)
1852	Lower Burma	Bengal	King of Ava
1854	Jhansi*	Bengal	Raja of Jhansi (death of)
1854	Nagpur*	Bengal	Raja of Nagpur (death of)
1856	Oudh	Bengal	King of Oudh (deposed)

* Assumed by Dalhousie's 'Doctrine of Lapse'

Table 2 – Major Wars and Battles of the EIC Armies

War	Enemy	Presidency	Date Range	Major Battles		
Maratha Skirmishes	Marathas	Bo	1718-1722	Gheria 1718	Kolaba 1721	
First Carnatic War	French	Ma	1746-1748	Fort St. George 1746	Pondicherry 1748	
Carnatic 'Adventures'	French	Ma	1751-1752	Arcot 1751	Trichinopoly 1751	Srirangam 1752
Maratha Skirmishes	Marathas	Bo	1755-1756	Savandurga 1755	Gheria 1756	
Bengal War	Nawab of Bengal	Be	1756-1757	Calcutta 1757	Chittoor 1757	Plassey 1757
Seven Years' War	French	Be/Ma	1756-1763	Chandernagore 1757	Trichinopoly 1758	Pondicherry 1761
Bengal Campaign	Nawab of Bengal	Be	1763-1764	Gheria 1763	Katwa 1763	Buxar 1764
First Mysore War	Sultan of Mysore	Ma	1767	Changama 1767	Trinomalai (Tiruvannamalai) 1767	
Second Mysore War	Sultan of Mysore	Ma	1779-1784	Perambakkam 1780	Porto Novo 1781	Sholinghur 1781
First Maratha War	Marathas	Bo	1779-1780	Wadgaon (Wargaum) 1779	Gwalior 1780	Gujarat 1780
Third Mysore War	Sultan of Mysore	Ma	1790-1792	Calicut 1790	Nandidroog 1791,	Savandurga 1791
Fourth Mysore War	Sultan of Mysore	Ma	1799-1800	Sedasseer 1799	Mallavalli 1799	Seringapatam 1799
Second Maratha War	Marathas	Ma	1803-1805	Ahmadnagar 1803	Assaye 1803	Argaon 1803
Second Maratha War	Marathas	Be	1803-1805	Laswari 1803	Farrukhabad 1804	Bharatpur 1805
Nepalese War	Gurkhas	Be	1814-1816	Kalanga 1814	Jaitak 1815	Malaun 1815
Third Maratha War	Marathas	Bo/Ma	1817-1818	Kirkee 1817	Sitabaldi 1817	Koregaon 1818
First Burma War	Burmese	Be/Ma	1824-1826	Kemmendine 1824	Prome 1825	Pagan 1826
First Afghan War	Afghans	Be	1839-1842	Ghazni 1839	Gandamak 1842	Jalalabad 1842
First China War	Chinese	Ma	1840-1842	Canton 1841	Shanghai 1842	Chinkiang 1842
Sind War	Baluchis	Bo	1843	Hyderabad (Sind) 1843	Miani 1843	
Gwalior	Marathas	Be	1843	Maharajpur 1843	Panniar 1843	
Baluchistan	Baluchis	Bo	1845	Traki 1845		
First Sikh War	Sikhs	Be	1845-1846	Mudki 1845	Aliwal 1846	Sobraon 1846
Second Sikh War	Sikhs	Be	1846-1849	Multan 1848	Chilianwala 1849	Gujrat 1849
Second Burma War	Burmese	Ma	1852-1853	Martaban 1852	Prome 1852	Toungoo 1853
Second China War	Chinese	Ma	1856-1858	Canton 1857	Taku Forts 1858	Palikao 1860
Indian Mutiny	Rebel Sepoys	Be	1857-1858	Delhi 1857	Lucknow 1857	Jhansi 1858

This Table provides a list of major wars, and up to three of the more important battles in each war undertaken by the Company's Armies from 1718 to 1861. The list is limited to enable it to fit onto a single page and excluded battles of major wars would eclipse some of those listed for the smaller wars. So this list by no means paints a complete picture of the total activities of these three armies.

Table 3 – Development of EIC Armies' Structure 1795 - 1857

Bengal	Regiments/Battalions	1795	Numbers in: 1824	1857
Gov.-General's Troops				2
Cavalry	Regiments/Troop	4/6	8	10/6
Horse Artillery	Brigade/Troops	-	1/7	2/4+1/5
Foot Artillery				
- European	Battalions/Companies	3/5	3/8	6/4+
- Native	Battalions/Companies	-	1/20	3/6+
Engineers	Battalions		1	5
Sappers/Miners (Pioneers)	Companies		-	1/12
Infantry				
- European	Regiments/Companies [or Wings]	3	7	3/10+3/[2]
- Native	Regiments/Battalions/Companies	12/2/10	69	74/10
Invalids (Veterans)	Regiments	1	3	5
Pensioners		-	1	-
Town Major's List		-	1	1

+ 1 mixed Battalion.

Madras		1795	1824	1857
Cavalry	Regiments/Troops	4/6	8	8/6+
Horse Artillery	Brigades/Troops	-	2/4	1/6
Foot Artillery				
- European	Battalions/Companies	2/5	3/4	4/4
- Native	Battalions/Companies	-	1/4	1/6
Engineers	Corps/Battalions	1	1	1/3
Sappers/Miners (Pioneers)	Regiments	1	1	1/9
Infantry				
- European	Regiments	2	2	3/10
- Native	Regiments/Battalions/Companies	10/2/10	52	52/10
Invalids (Veterans)	Regiments		1	3
Pensioners		#	1	-
Effective Supernumeraries		-	1	1

Not organized into Regiments   + and 1 Troop for the Governor.

Bombay		1795	1824	1857
Cavalry	Regiments/Troops	-	3	3/6+
Horse Artillery	Brigades/Troops	-	2/2	1/4
Foot Artillery				
- European	Battalions/Companies	1/5	1	2/4
- Native	Battalions/Companies	-	1/4	2/6
Engineers	Corps	1	1	1/3
Sappers/Miners (Pioneers)	Regiments	-	1	1/5
Infantry				
- European	Regiments/Companies	1	3	3/10
- Native	Regiments/Battalions	4/2	24	29/10
Invalids (Veterans)	Regiments	3	1	1
Pensioners		-		3
Town Major's List		-	1	1

+ and 1 Troop for Governor.

Table 4 – Composition of the major Units of the EIC Armies - 1857

Service	Bengal	Madras	Bombay
Light Cavalry	Governor-General's Bodyguard 2 Troops	Governor's Bodyguard 1 Troop	Governor's Bodyguard 1 Troop
	10 Native Regts 6 Troops each	8 Native Regts 6 Troops each	3 Native Regts 6 Troops each
Infantry	3 European Regts 10 Companies ea.	3 European Regts 10 Companies ea.	3 European Regts 10 Companies ea.
	74 Native Regts 10 Companies ea.	52 Native Regts 10 Companies ea.	29 Native Regts 10 Companies ea.
Horse Artillery	3 Brigades -1 of 5 Troops (3 Eur & 2 Nat) plus -2 of 4 Troops (3 European & 1 Native)	1 Brigade of 6 Troops (4 European & 2 Native)	1 Brigade of 4 Troops (2 European & 2 Native)
Foot Artillery	9 Battalions -6 of 4 European Cos. -2 of 6 Native Cos. -1 of 4 Eur & 3 Nat. Cos.	5 Battalions -4 of 4 Europ. Cos. -1 of 6 Native Cos.	4 Battalions -2 of 4 Eur. Cos. -2 of 6 Nat. Cos.
Engineers	5 Battalions	3 Battalions	3 Battalions
Sappers and Miners	12 Companies	9 Companies	5 Companies
Invalids (Veterans)	5 Battalions -1 European Infantry -2 Native Artillery -2 Native Infantry	3 Battalions -1 European plus -2 Native each of -1 Artillery Co. & -1 Infantry Co.	2 Battalions Each of 2 Cos. (1 Eur. & 1 Nat.) 1 Native Battalion of 8 Companies

In addition, each Presidency had many officers and soldiers allocated to non-fighting Departments or units such as: Commissariat, Ordnance Commissariat, Paymaster, Quartermaster General, Pensions, Gun Carriage, Gunpowder, Public Works and Judge Advocate General. No separate section makes reference to the 'Town Major's List' in the Presidency Army Lists but the relevant soldiers are numbered in the various fighting and non-fighting units.

Note: The data for Tables 4 to 4D were taken from the Presidency Army Lists.

Table 4A - Composition of the EIC Cavalry Regiments – 1857*

Native Cavalry		European Cavalry*	
Colonels	1	Colonels	1
Lieut. Cols.	1	Lieutenant Colonels	2
Majors	1	Majors	2
Captains	7	Captains	14
Lieutenants	9	Lieutenants	18
Cornets	4	Cornets	8
Adjutant	1	Adjutant	1
Quartermaster and Interpreter	1	Quartermaster and Interpreter	1
Surgeons	1	Surgeons	1
Assistant Surgeons		Assistant Surgeons	2
Subadar Major		Veterinary Surgeons	2
Riding Masters	1	Riding Masters	2
No. of Troops per Regiment	**6**	**No. of Troops per Regiment**	**10**

Soldiers per Regiment		Soldiers per Regiment	
Sergeant-Major	1	Riding Master	1
Quarter-Master Sergeant	1	Regimental Serjeant Major	1
Assistant Apothecary	1	Troop Serjeant Majors	10
Second Dresser	1	Quarter-Master Serjeant	1
Subadars	6	Armourer Serjeant	1
Jemadars	6	Saddler Serjeant	1
Havildar-Major	1	Farrier Serjeant	1
Havildars	30	Hospital Serjeant	1
Naigues	24	Orderly Room Clerk	1
Trumpet Major	1	Serjeants	40
Trumpeters	6	Trumpet Major	1
Farrier Major	1	Trumpeters	10
Farriers	12	Corporals	40
Veterinary Pupils	2	Farriers	10
Troopers	300	Privates	700
Recruit and Pension Boys	40		
Second Tindal	1		
Regimental Lascars	8		
Choudry	1		
Peons	2		
Puckallies	6		
Artificers	5		
Toties	2		

* Source: Presidency Army Lists for 1857.

Note: The Bengal Native Cavalry were among the first to mutiny in 1857 and were soon disbanded. Five Regiments of European Cavalry were established in 1858 and later reduced to three after the mutiny had been quelled. They were then transferred to serve in the British Army. The data for the European Cavalry therefore apply to 1859.

Table 4B – Composition of EIC Artillery Corps

Presidency Artillery Corps

Colonels	7
Lieut. Cols.	8
Majors	8
Captains	42
Lieutenants	70
2nd. Lieutenants	42
Assistant Adjutants General	2
Adjutants & Quartermasters	7
Adjutants	2
Quartermaster & Interpreter	2
Surgeons	6
Assistant Surgeons	15
Veterinary Surgeons	2
Riding Master	1
Subadar Major	1

Each Troop/Coy HQ	Horse	Foot
Riding Master	1	-
Sergeant-Major	1	1
Quarter-Master Sergeant	1	1
School Master Serjeant	1	1
Drill Serjeant		1
Orderly Room Clerk		1
Trumpet Major	1	1
Farrier Major	1	
2nd Apothecary		1
Assistant Apothecary		1
Second Dresser		1
Drill Corporal		1
Bugle Major		1
Lascar Boys		16

European Artillery

No of Troops per Brigade 10
No of Companies per Battalion 4

No. of Soldiers per	Horse Troop	Foot Coy
Quarter-Master		1
Serjeant-Major		1
Quarter-Master Serjeant	1	
Brigade Staff Serjeant		1
Sergeants	6	6
Corporals	6	6
Bombardiers	12	6
Trumpeters	2	
Buglers		2
Half-pay Buglers	2	
Farriers	3	
Gunners	84	60
Assistant Apothecary		1
Second Dresser		1
Puckallies	4	2
Artificers		12
Horses	64	

Note: Variations occur by Presidency
* Figures provided for a Battalion only.

Source: Presidency Army Lists 1857

Native Artillery

Extra Horse Battery HQ Staff

Rough Rider	1	Havildars	2
Farrier Serjt	1	Naigues	2
Asst. Farrier & Saddler Serjt.	1		

No of Troops per Brigade 10
No of Companies per Battalion 6

No. of Soldiers per	Horse Troop	Foot Coy
Subadars	1	1
Jemadars	1	2
Quarter-Master	1	1*
Serjeant-Major	1	1*
Quarter-Master Serjeant	1	1*
Serjeants		3
Assistant Apothecary		1
Havildar-Major		1
Drill Havildar		1
Havildars		8
Drill Naigues	1	1*
Trumpeters/Buglers	2	2
Farriers	3	
Veterinary Pupil	1	
Troopers/Privates	84	88
Puckallies	3	1
Recruit Boys	5	5
Pension Boys	3	7
Regimental Lascars	2	3
Artificers	12	
Horses	150	

Table 4C – Composition of a Regiment of Infantry and of Sappers and Miners*

per Regiment of:	Infantry		Sappers and Miners
	European	Native	
Colonels	1	1	(Many Officers were
Lieut. Cols.	2	1	Taken from Infantry
Majors	2	1	and Engineers)
Captains	14	7	1
Lieutenants	22	11	22
2nd. Lieutenants	10		
Ensigns	4		Conductor 1
Adjutant	1	1	1
Quartermaster and Interpreter	1	1	1
Surgeons	2	1	
Assistant Surgeons	2	1	
Subadar Major			
No. of Companies per Regiment	**10**	**10**	**9**
No. of Soldiers per Regiment			
Sergeant-Major	1	1	1
Quarter-Master Sergeant	1	1	1
Staff Sergeants	4		
Sergeants	50		18
Corporals	50		36
Drum or Bugle Major	1		
Drummers or Buglers	20	20	18
Half-pay Drummers/Buglers	20		
Privates (E) or Sepoys (N)	800	700	1039
2nd Apothecary	1		1
Assistant Apothecary	1	1	1
Second Dresser	1	1	1
Hospital Writer	1		
Subadars		10	9
Jemadars		10	9
Havildar-Major		1	1
Havildars		50	38
Naigues		50	76
Recruit Boys	30		24
Pension Boys	40		
Artificers	3	4	43
Puckallies (Water Carriers)	20	10	
Peons	2		
Bahadoor	1		

* Source: Presidency Army Lists for 1857.

Note: The actual numbers varied a little with Presidency and date.

Table 4D – Composition of Further Units of the EIC Armies in 1857*

The Commissariat

	Bengal	Madras	Bombay
Army Commissariat Department			
Commissary General	1	1	1
Deputy Commissary General	2	1	1
Assistant Commissary General	6	6	3
Deputy Assistant Commissary General	8	8	3
Sub-Assistant Commissary General	18	12	8
Probationary Sub-Assistant Commissary General			5
Deputy Commissary	1		1
Assistant Commissary	2		1
Deputy Assistant Commissary	2	2	3
Acting Commissariat Agent Class 1			3
Acting Commissariat Agent Class 2			2
Conductor	10	8	6
Sub-Conductor	15	11	9
Ordnance Commissariat Department			
Inspector General of Ordnance and Magazines	1		
Principal Commissary of Ordnance	1	1	1
Deputy Principal Commissary of Ordnance			3
Commissary of Ordnance	6	7	4
Deputy Commissary of Ordnance	11	5	3
Assistant Commissary of Ordnance	9	3	1
Deputy Assistant Commissary of Ordnance	4	7	4
Conductor (or Troop Quartermaster) of Ordnance	72	41	22
Conductor at Gun Carriage Manufactory		1	1
Sub-Conductor of Ordnance	33	42	33
Officiating Conductor of Ordnance	31		
Officiating Sub-Conductor of Ordnance	2		
Sub-Conductor at Gun Carriage Manufactory		2	2

* Source: Presidency Army Lists for 1857.

Note: The actual numbers varied a little with Presidency and date.

Table 5 - Transfer of East India Company Forces
to the British Army in 1861

A. Cavalry

HEIC Regiment	became in British Army
1st Bengal European Light Cavalry	19th Hussars
2nd Bengal European Light Cavalry	20th Hussars
3rd Bengal European Light Cavalry	21st Hussars

B. Infantry

HEIC Regiment	became	and later
1st Bengal Fusiliers	H.M. 101st Regt.	1st Royal Munster Fusiliers
2nd Bengal Fusiliers	H.M. 104th Regt.	2nd Royal Munster Fusiliers
3rd Bengal Light Infantry	H.M. 107th Regt.	2nd Royal Sussex Regiment

4th, 5th and 6th Bengal European Regiments, formed in 1858, were retained as 'Cadres' only until disbanded in 1867/8

1st Madras Fusiliers	H.M. 102nd Regt.	1st Royal Dublin Fusiliers
2nd Madras Light Infantry	H.M. 105th Regt	2nd Kings Own Yorkshire Lt. Inf.
3rd Madras Infantry	H.M. 108th Regt.	2nd Royal Inniskilling Fusiliers.
1st Bombay Fusiliers	H.M. 103rd Regt.	2nd Royal Dublin Fusiliers
2nd Bombay Light Infantry	H.M. 106th Regt.	2nd Durham Light Infantry
3rd Bombay Regiment	H.M. 109th Regt.	2nd Leinster Regiment

Alternatively

New British Regiment	Formerly in HEIC Army
H.M. 101st Regiment	1st Bengal Fusiliers
H.M. 102nd Regiment	1st Madras Fusiliers
H.M. 103rd Regiment	1st Bombay Fusiliers
H.M. 104th Regiment	2nd Bengal Fusiliers
H.M. 105th Regiment	2nd Madras Light Infantry
H.M. 106th Regiment	2nd Bombay Light Infantry
H.M. 107th Regiment	3rd Bengal Light Infantry
H.M. 108th Regiment	3rd Madras Infantry
H.M. 109th Regiment	3rd Bombay Regiment

Table 5 (continued) - Transfer of EIC Forces to the British Army in 1861

C. Horse Artillery

Former Troop (Europeans in HEIC)			became (in Royal Horse Artillery)	
Bengal	1st Troop	1st Brigade	'A' Battery	2nd Brigade
Bengal	1st Troop	2nd Brigade	'A' Battery	5th Brigade
Bengal	1st Troop	3rd Brigade	'F' Battery	2nd Brigade
Bengal	2nd Troop	1st Brigade	'B' Battery	2nd Brigade
Bengal	2nd Troop	2nd Brigade	'B' Battery	5th Brigade
Bengal	2nd Troop	3rd Brigade	'G' Battery	2nd Brigade
Bengal	3rd Troop	1st Brigade	'C' Battery	2nd Brigade
Bengal	3rd Troop	2nd Brigade	'C' Battery	5th Brigade
Bengal	3rd Troop	3rd Brigade	'E' Battery	5th Brigade
Bengal	4th Troop	1st Brigade	'D' Battery	2nd Brigade
Bengal	4th Troop	2nd Brigade	'D' Battery	5th Brigade
Bengal	4th Troop	3rd Brigade	'F' Battery	5th Brigade
Bengal	5th Troop	1st Brigade	'E' Battery	2nd Brigade
Madras	'A' Troop	1st Brigade	'A' Battery	3rd Brigade
Madras	'B' Troop	1st Brigade	'B' Battery	3rd Brigade
Madras	'C' Troop	1st Brigade	'C' Battery	3rd Brigade
Madras	'D' Troop	1st Brigade	'D' Battery	3rd Brigade
Madras	'E' Troop	1st Brigade	Disbanded	
Bombay	1st Troop		'A' Battery	4th Brigade
Bombay	2nd Troop		'B' Battery	4th Brigade
Bombay	3rd Troop		'C' Battery	4th Brigade
Bombay	4th Troop		'D' Battery	4th Brigade

D. Foot Artillery

Former Companies (Europeans in HEIC)		became (in Royal Artillery)	
Bengal	1st to 4th Companies, 1st Battalion	1st to 4th Batteries	16th Brigade
Bengal	1st to 4th Companies, 2nd Battalion	1st to 4th Batteries	19th Brigade
Bengal	1st to 4th Companies, 3rd Battalion	1st to 4th Batteries	22nd Brigade
Bengal	1st to 4th Companies, 4th Battalion	1st to 4th Batteries	24th Brigade
Bengal	1st to 4th Companies, 5th Battalion	1st to 4th Batteries	25th Brigade
Bengal	1st to 4th Companies, 6th Battalion	5th Battery of 16th, 19th, 22nd, 24th	Brigades respectively
Madras	'A' to 'D' Companies, 1st Battalion	1st to 4th Batteries	17th Brigade
Madras	'A' to 'D' Companies, 2nd Battalion	1st to 4th Batteries	20th Brigade
Madras	'A' to 'D' Companies, 3rd Battalion	1st to 4th Batteries	23rd Brigade
Madras	'A' Company, 4th Battalion	5th Battery	17th Brigade
Madras	'B' Company, 4th Battalion	6th Battery	17th Brigade
Madras	'C' Company, 4th Battalion	5th Battery	20th Brigade
Madras	'D' Company, 4th Battalion	5th Battery	23rd Brigade
Bombay	1st to 4th Companies, 1st Battalion	1st to 4th Batteries	18th Brigade
Bombay	1st to 4th Companies, 2nd Battalion	1st to 4th Batteries	21st Brigade
Bombay	1st to 2nd Companies, Reserve Artillery	5th & 6th Batteries	18th Brigade
Bombay	3rd to 4th Companies, Reserve Artillery	5th & 6th Batteries	21st Brigade

Table 6 – Divisional Headquarters of the East India Company's Armies (1857)

Source: Presidency Army Lists for 1857. The spellings of the various locations are those commonly used by the British Authorities in the mid-nineteenth century and may differ from those used in the twentieth century and today

Bengal		Madras		Bombay	
Division	**Headquarters**	**Division**	**Headquarters**	**Division**	**Headquarters**
Presidency	Barrackpore	Central	Presidency	Northern	Ahmedabad
Cawnpore	Cawnpore	Southern	Trichinopoly	Poona	Poona
Dinapore	Dinapore	Northern	Vizagapatam	Southern	Belgaum
Meerut	Meerut	Malabar and Canara	Cannanore	Scinde	Kurrachee
Rohilcund	Bareilly	Nagpore	Kamptee	Rajputana	Nusseerabad
Gwalior Contingent	Gwalior	Mysore	Bangalore		
Sirhind	Umballah	Ceded Districts	Bellary		
Lahore	Lahore	Hyderabad Subsidiary Force	Secunderabad		
Peshawur	Peshawur	Saugor*	Saugor		
Sind Sagur	Rawul Pindee	Straits**	Singapore		
Pegu**	Rangoon				

* Transferred to Bengal in 1857

** Reported to Bengal but garrisoned by forces of the Madras Presidency

List of Principal Sources

(Abbreviations: Be=Bengal; Ma = Madras; Bo = Bombay)

IOR Reference	Content	Dates	Page
Z/L/MIL/5/16-43	Registers of Soldiers' References	1860-1873	83
Z/L/MIL/9/1	Index to Cadet Papers	1789-1860	14
Z/L/MIL/9/5	Nominal Index of Asst. Surgeons	1804-1854	17
Z/L/MIL/10/1	Index to Officers' Services – Be	1759-1858	19, 20
Z/L/MIL/10/2	Officers' pre-furlough Services – Be	1860-1892	23, 25
Z/L/MIL/10/3-4	Officers' Retirement Certificate Index	1836-1896	58
Z/L/MIL/11/1	Index to Officers' Services – Ma	1762-1859	19, 20
Z/L/MIL/11/2	Officers' pre-furlough Services – Ma	1860-1892	25
Z/L/MIL/12/1	Index to Officers' Services – Bo	1753-1859	19, 20
Z/L/MIL/12/2	Officers' pre-furlough Services – Bo	1860-1892	25
L/MIL/3	Military Despatches	1803-1907	82-83
L/MIL/5/42-314	Medal, Prize and Batta Rolls	1799-1861	68
L/MIL/5/362-375	Soldiers' References	1860-1873	83
L/MIL/9/1-28	Registers of Recruits	1817-1860	35
L/MIL/9/29-45	Depot Description Lists	1801-1860	36
L/MIL/9/77-102	Embarkation Lists	1824-1860	37-39
L/MIL/9/107-253, 255-291, 358-408	Papers and Registers relating to Cadets and Assistant Surgeons	1789-1861	14-18
L/MIL/9/433-434	Papers relating to Veterinary Surgeons	1826-1859	18
L/MIL/10/1-19	Be Army Lists (1)	1781-1849	27
L/MIL/10/20-98	Be Officers' Services	1770-1892	20-21, 23-25
L/MIL/10/104-107	Be Officers' Casualty Returns	1824-1895	26
L/MIL/10/108-112	Officers' Retirement Certificates All	1836-1857	58
L/MIL/10/122-129	Be Soldiers' Records	1793-1860	42
L/MIL/10/130-200	Be Muster Rolls and Casualty Returns	1716-1865	44-45
L/MIL/10/301-302	Soldiers' Discharge All Presidencies	1830-1882	50
L/MIL/10/303-317	Be Post-Mutiny Discharge Papers	1859-1861	51-52
L/MIL/10/324-326	Be Soldiers Transfer to British Army	1858-1860	54
L/MIL/11/1-37	Ma Army Lists (1)	1759-1846	27
L/MIL/11/38-92	Ma Officers' Services	1762-1892	20, 22, 24-25
L/MIL/11/93-98	Ma Officers' Casualty Returns	1800-1895	26
L/MIL/11/101-108	Ma Soldiers' Records	1793-1860	42
L/MIL/11/109-276	Ma Muster Rolls and Casualty Returns	1762-1907	44, 46
L/MIL/11/278-281	Ma Post-Mutiny Discharge Papers	1859-1861	52
L/MIL/11/282	Ma Soldiers Transfer to British Army	1858-1860	54
L/MIL/12/1-17-66	Bo Army Lists (1) plus Duplicates	1759-1855	27
L/MIL/12/67-101	Bo Officers' Services	1770-1892	20, 22, 24-25
L/MIL/12/102-105	Bo Officers' Casualty Returns	1844-1895	26
L/MIL/12/109-116	Bo Soldiers' Records	1793-1860	42
L/MIL/12/117-265	Bo Muster Lists and Casualty Returns	1708-1907	44, 46
L/MIL/12/282-286	Bo Post-Mutiny Discharge Papers	1859-1861	52
L/MIL/12/288	Bo Soldiers Transfer to British Army	1858-1860	54

IOR Reference	Content	Dates	Page
L/MIL/13/1-15	St Helena Muster Lists	1789-1834	9
L/MIL/14/1-49	Summary Service Records	1892-1916	25
L/MIL/14/214-215	Brief Recruitment and Service Details	1896	37
L/MIL/14/239-	Later Summary Service Records	post-1892	25
L/MIL/17/2/1-267	Bengal Army Lists (2)	1819-1889	28
L/MIL/17/2/269-352	Bengal General Orders	1820-1862+	81
L/MIL/17/3/1-329	Madras Army Lists (2)	1810-1895	28
L/MIL/17/3/335-426	Madras General Orders	1800-1860+	81
L/MIL/17/4/1-362	Bombay Army Lists (2)	1823-1895	28
L/MIL/17/4/363-467	Bombay General Orders	1820-1860+	81
Z/L/AG/34/1-2	Early Wills Index	1618-1779	79
Z/L/AG/34/4-5	Be General Administrations Index	1741-1909	79
Z/L/AG/34/6-7	Be General Wills Index	1780-1908	79
Z/L/AG/34/8-9	Ma General Wills and Admons. Index	1780-1908	79
Z/L/AG/34/10	Bo General Wills and Admons. Index	1776-1909	79
Z/L/AG/34/12	District Court Wills and Admons	post-1865	79
Z/L/AG/34/17-21	Indexes to Treasury Deposits	1792-1919	80
L/AG/9/4/1-12	Warrant Payment Authorities'	1788-1860	58
L/AG/9/4/28-30	Officers' & Widows' Pension Payments	1849-1860	59
L/AG/21/10/4-41	Officers' & Widows' Pension Payments	1820-1893	59
L/AG/21/11/1-18	Pension Payments Officers in Europe	1825-1860	59
L/AG/21/12/1-46	Colonel's Allowances	1803-1948	56, 57
L/AG/21/26/1-18	Family Pension Funds - UK Payment	1842-1900	60-62
L/AG/21/27/4-5	Be Orphans' Payment Books	1881-1886	57, 62
L/AG/21/29/1-41	Ma Medical Fund Payments	1849-1955	57, 61
L/AG/21/30/1-2, 10-20	Ma Military Fund Payments	1881-1903	57, 61
L/AG/21/32/1, 8-31	Bo Military Fund UK Payments	1851-1946	62
L/AG/21/44/1-7	Pension Payments in Colonies	1859-1928+	57, 66
L/AG/23/2/20-40	Soldiers' Pension Applications/Payments	1772-1798	63, 64
L/AG/23/2/41-69	Soldiers' Pension Pay'ts/Admissions	1779-1882	63, 65
L/AG/23/6/1-19	Be Officers' Pension Records	1824-1938	26, 60
L/AG/23/7/2-20	Be Military Orphans' Society Records	1818-1950	49, 62
L/AG/23/9/1-3	Ma Medical Fund Administration	1870-1881	61
L/AG/23/10/1-2, 10-19	Ma Officers' Pension Records	1808-1913	26, 60, 61
L/AG/23/12/6	Bo Military Fund Subscribers' Lists	1858, 66, 75	62
L/AG/23/12/1-4	Bo Officers' Pension Contributions	1816-1862	26
L/AG/23/12/10-12	Bo Military Fund UK Payments	1866-1881	62
L/AG/34/29/1-380	Be/Ma/Bo Court Records (Wills, &c.)	1774-1937	79
L/AG/34/30/1-29	Soldiers' (and Officers') Wills	1838-1862	77
L/AG/34/31/1-21	District Court Records (Wills. &c.)	post-1865	79
L/AG/35/50-54	Summary Soldiers' Pension Records	1829-1881	57, 64, 66

Glossary of Military Ranks and Terms

**Ranks of Officers
(of increasing importance)**

- Cadet
- Ensign (Infantry), Cornet (Cavalry)
- Lieutenant Fireworker
  (Artillery pre-1819)
- Third Lieutenant
  (From c1760 to c1790)
- Subaltern (or Second Lieutenant)
- Lieutenant
- Captain Lieutenant (to 1785)
- Captain
- Major
- Lieutenant-Colonel
- Colonel
- Brigadier-General
- Major-General
- Lieutenant-General
- General

**Ranks of Soldiers
(of increasing importance)**

- Private (Infantry, Dragoons)
- Matross (Junior Gunner in Artillery
  discontinued in 1824)
- Gunner (Artillery)
- Trooper (Lancers, Hussars)
- Corporal (Infantry, Dragoons, Senior
  Gunner in Artillery)
- Bombardier (Senior Howitzer Gunner in
  Artillery)
- Serjeant (see below for types of Serjeant
  in Town Major's List)
- Quartermaster Serjeant
- Colour Serjeant
- Serjeant-Major
- Quartermaster Serjeant-Major
- Sub-Conductor (Warrant Officer)
- Conductor (Warant Officer)

Note the spelling of Serjeant with a 'j'
as generally used by the EIC Armies

Town Major's List (called 'Effective Supernumeraries' in Madras Presidency)

After a number of years in the Infantry or Artillery, certain soldiers were selected to serve in the "Town Major's List", known in Madras as the "Effective Supernumeraries". Their function was to provide a variety of support services, particularly Commissariat and Ordnance, to the active units. A small number of these soldiers were ranked as Private or Corporal but the majority were ranked as Serjeant, according to the function for which they were engaged. Although their precise functions are not recorded, these included:

Serjeant-Major	Barrack Serjeant	Road Serjeant
Garrison Serjeant-Major	Overseer Serjeant	Saluting Serjeant
Cantonment Serjeant-Major	Hospital Serjeant	Signal Serjeant
Engineering Serjeant- Major	Key Serjeant	Store Serjeant
Serjeant Instructor	Laboratory Serjeant	
Arrack Godown Serjeant	Commissariat Staff Serjeant	

As he became more senior, a Non-Commissioned Officer (NCO) in the East India Company Army could be promoted to the rank of Warrant Officer, firstly as a Sub-Conductor and later as full Conductor. Beyond this, a number of senior Warrant Officers were promoted to the ranks of 'Honorary Lieutenant' then 'Honorary Captain' and, in very limited cases, even to 'Honorary Major' and 'Honorary Lieut. Colonel. These positions were almost exclusively in the 'Commissariat', 'Ordnance', 'Barracks' or the 'Public Works' Departments.

Native Military Ranks

Ranks of Indian Officers and Soldiers	Approximate Equivalent British Rank

Cavalry*

Rissaldar-Major	Captain
Rissaldar	First Lieutenant
Ressaidar	Senior Second Lieutenant
Jemadar	Second Lieutenant
Kot Daffadar	Troop Serjeant-Major
Daffadar	Serjeant
Lance-Daffadar	Corporal
Acting Lance-Daffadar	Lance-Corporal
Sowar	Trooper

Infantry

Subadar-Major	Captain
Subadar	First Lieutenant
Jemadar	Second Lieutenant
Havildar-Major	Serjeant-Major
Havildar	Serjeant
Naigue or Naik	Corporal
Lance-Naigue	Lance-Corporal
Sepoy	Private

General

Tindal	Foreman (generally in Ordnance Departments)
Lascar	Worker (generally in the army); seaman
Choudry	Foreman (generally for Regimental Support)
Peons	'Runner' or Man available for menial duties.
Puckallies	Water Carriers
Toties	Messengers
Golundauze	The Native Battalions of Artillery

* The Native Cavalry used the same nomenclature for their Officers and NCOs as the Native Infantry until the re-organization of 1860. The use of the ranks cited above had earlier been used by the Irregular Cavalry, however.

A Few Useful Explanations and Abbreviations from Military records

Batta	A special allowance made to officers and soldiers whilst in the field or on the march.
E.V.B.	European Veterans Battalion (CEVB = Carnatic European Veterans Battalion)
GOG.	General Orders by Governor
GOCC	General Orders by Commander-in-Chief
S.C	Sick Certificate
P.A.	Private Affairs
P.	Passed District Examination in the Persian and Hindoostanee Languages
P.H.	Passed District Examination in the Hindoostanee Language

Specialist Military Terms

Brevet.   An officer was generally promoted within the corps in which he served in accordance with his seniority and any vacancy within that corps due to transfer, retirement or death. Certain officers were, however, deemed worthy of a higher rank by virtue of long and/or distinguished service but were unable to be granted it due to the lack of vacancy. Accordingly, a Commander-in-Chief was empowered to issue a letter (French word, 'Brevet') granting him 'Brevet' Rank within the Army at large. Generally, this conferred with it the uniform and right to command of the 'higher' rank.

Dragoon.   A mounted soldier whose weapon was a 'Dragoon' or short musket. Note that Officers and soldiers on the Dragoons used ranks of the Infantry regiments.

Hussar   A Cavalryman generally armed with a Sabre.

Lancer.   A Cavalryman armed with a Lance.

Regiment.   A group of about 500 officers and soldiers under the charge of a Colonel. After 1879, in the British Army most regiments comprised two Battalions, each of 500 men or so, one under the charge of a Colonel and the other of a Lieutenant-Colonel. In theory, one Battalion was to remain in England, recruiting and training, whilst the other served abroad.

Battalion.   A group of about 500 men under the command of a Colonel, often a titular role only, and led by a Lieutenant-Colonel. It generally comprised a 'Headquarters' Company, plus 2 to 5 other Companies

Troop   A unit of about 100 mounted Cavalrymen or gunners of Horse Artillery, generally under the command of a Captain.

Company.   A unit of about 100 men, usually under the charge of a Captain. Note that the several Companies of Artillery were normally posted to geographically separate stations.

Platoon.   In the 18th century a Regiment comprised approximately 20 Platoons of 24 men each, between 2 and 4 of which were 'Grenadiers' (Infantry) or of Light Cavalry (Cavalry). The term Platoon was rarely used in the 19th century but revived in the 20th century.

Wing.   An infantry regiment generally comprised two 'Wings' of 8 Companies each, commonly referred to as the 'Left Wing' and the 'Right Wing'.

Note that, particularly with effect from a law introduced in 1795, the East India Company's Armies followed the same ranking, structures, procedures and disciplines as the British Army. Their officers held their commissions from the Crown.